D1594397

Education
and Philosophical
Anthropology

Also by David Holbrook:

POETRY

Imaginings
Against the Cruel Frost
Object-Relations
Old World New World
Chance of a Lifetime
Selected Poems

NOVELS

Flesh Wounds
A Play of Passion
Nothing Larger Than Life

ON EDUCATION

English for Maturity
English for the Rejected
The Secret Places
The Exploring Word
Children's Writing
English in Australia Now
English for Meaning

CRITICISM

The Quest for Love
Human Hope and the Death Instinct
The Masks of Hate
Sex and Dehumanisation
Dylan Thomas: The Code of Night
The Pseudo-Revolution
Gustav Mahler and the Courage To Be
The Case Against Pornography (Ed.)
Sylvia Plath: Poetry and Existence
Lost Bearings in English Poetry
Education, Nihilism and Survival
Evolution and the Humanities
Authenticity and the Novel

Education
and Philosophical
Anthropology

Toward a New View of Man for the Humanities and English

David Holbrook

Rutherford • Madison • Teaneck
Fairleigh Dickinson University Press
London and Toronto: Associated University Presses

© 1987 by Associated University Presses, Inc.

Associated University Presses
440 Forsgate Drive
Cranbury, NJ 08512

Associated University Presses
25 Sicilian Avenue
London WC1A 2QH, England

Associated University Presses
2133 Royal Windsor Drive
Unit 1
Mississauga, Ontario
Canada L5J 1K5

The paper used in this publication meets the requirements
of the American National Standard for Permanence of Paper
for Printed Library Materials Z39.48-1984.

Library of Congress Cataloging-in-Publication Data

Holbrook, David.
  Education and philosophical anthropology.

  Bibliography: p.
  Includes index.
  1. Philosophical anthropology.   2. Knowledge,
Theory of.   3. Ethics.   I. Title.
BD450.H617   1987   128   85-45787
ISBN 0-8386-3275-0 (alk. paper)

Printed in the United States of America

For Frederick and Judith Tomlin

Was kann ich wissen?
Was soll ich tun?
Was darf ich hoffen?
Was ist der Mensch?
Immanuel Kant

Contents

Acknowledgments

The author wishes to express his gratitude to the Elmgrant Trust at Dartington Hall, to the Arts Council of Great Britain, and to Downing College, for support during the composition of this work.

For permission to quote from published material acknowledgment is made to the following: from *Collected Papers* by D. W. Winnicott, by permission of Mark Paterson on behalf of the Winnicott Trust; from *Love and Will* by Rollo May, by permission of W. W. Norton and Company, Inc., Copyright (c) by W. W. Norton and Company, Inc., and by Souvenir Press, London; from *The Seventeenth Century Background* by Basil Willey, by permission of Chatto and Windus and the author's estate; from *The Knower and The Known* by Marjorie Grene, by permission of Faber and Faber, London; from Erwin Straus, *The Primary World of Senses,* The Free Press of Glencoe, by permission of the Macmillan Publishing Co.

Abbreviations Used for Key Works

AB *Approaches to a Philosophical Biology* (Marjorie Grene)
AH *Animal Nature and Human Nature* (W. H. Thorpe)
AR *Against Reductionism* (ed. Arthur Koestler and Robert Smithies)
BW *Being in the World* (Ludwig Binswanger)
CP *Collected Papers* (D. W. Winnicott)
EM *An Essay on Man* (Ernst Cassirer)
EN *Existential Neurosis* (E. K. Ledermann)
EP *The Eastern Philosophers* (E. W. F. Tomlin)
IU *The Idea of a University* (Karl Jaspers)
KK *The Knower and the Known* (Marjorie Grene)
LC "The Location of Culture" (in D. W. Winnicott, *Playing and Reality*)
LW *Love and Will* (Rollo May)
NK *New Knowledge in Human Values* (ed. Abraham Maslow)
PE *Philosophy is for Everyman* (Karl Jaspers)
PK *Personal Knowledge* (Michael Polanyi)
PP *Phenomenology in Psychiatry and Psychology* (Herbert Spiegelberg)
PS *The Primary World of Senses* (Erwin Straus)
TB *Towards a Psychology of Being* (Abraham Maslow)
TD *The Tacit Dimension* (Michael Polanyi)
TS *Towards Deep Subjectivity* (Roger Poole)

Education
and Philosophical
Anthropology

1

How Do We Know Man?

This book attempts to bring to the notice of students and teachers in education and the humanities a new area of thought about the nature of man and the nature of knowing, which has been seriously neglected.

While I call this field of thought new, I must admit that some impulses in this movement began over a hundred years ago. It is new in the sense that it is new to us, and this raises the question of paradigms, that is, the overall patterns of concepts and assumptions within which we do our work.

As I shall try to show, in certain disciplines there is a feeling that our paradigms are limiting: we cannot advance our knowledge until we find more profitable ones—until we find quite different perspectives in seeking to understand man, life, and the world, and until we develop a more adequate concept of what it is *to know*. The area of thought to which I attend here is called *philosophical anthropology*. Although some academics in Britain deny its existence, many respectable thinkers and writers use the term, as will appear—even though what kind of discipline it involves is not easy to define. *The Philosophy of Martin Buber* contains a chapter entitled "The Philosophical Anthropology . . ." and the term is also used by E. A. Burtt, Marjorie Grene, Ernst Cassirer, and Herbert Spiegelberg as well as by Gabriel Marcel, the French philosopher, so it offers us a good starting point.

Philosophical anthropology is a philosophical study of the nature of man. But it recognizes that man cannot be understood as we understand natural objects, that it, as long as we suppose that we can know natural objects only in an "objective" empirical way. Philosophical anthropology aims at description and insight, rather than the kind of deductive argument and analysis dominant in the natural sciences. It does not rely upon reduction, and it does not seek apodicity, that is, clear demonstration, in the Cartesian way. It is a phenomenological discipline, which means that it takes account of consciousness and its phenomena, and so must examine symbols and meanings—and, indeed, the whole of the subjective life.

To talk like this, of course, disturbs those trained in the scientific modes of the West, and to them it begins to smack of vagueness and wooliness, if not irrational nonsense. But this is itself a question of paradigms. For certain purposes science feels that it must reduce everything to matter in motion, and for examining the world in this way only measurements are real. As in the theories of Thomas Hobbes, the single source of knowledge about the world is sense: everything we know is fed in by the senses and retained in the memory. Science then imposes axioms upon the sensory base, in the hypothetico-deductive model of explanation. From these hypotheses science constructs explanations of a causal kind, in which given phenomena are shown to follow from certain causes. So the world is seen in terms of events, space-time coordinates, and ultimately the particles or waves specified in such terms. In our civilization, explanation is thought of in such reductive terms, and is hypothetico-deductive, materialistic and particulate: phenomena are to be understood in terms of the smallest components. As Marjorie Grene argues in a 1976 essay, "Hobbes and the Modern Mind" (*Philosophy in and out of Europe*, p. 155), this has led to a general feeling in our ways of thought that "there are only bodies moving and the analysis of their motion resolves these into parts. Nor, since all change is motion, can there be wholes not reducible to such least parts."

The general effect of these assumptions about what knowledge is and what there is to be known is to make us feel that the *real* is the physico-chemically real. It even seems to us that the advance of knowledge itself, enlightenment, lies in the reduction of everything to molecules and atoms. This, in turn, has a subtle but profound effect on our attitudes to life. Ironically, once life itself has been or soon will be, as we feel, explained away in terms of the nonliving, what is "real" comes to seem, by definition, the nonliving. And this has both a metaphysical and a moral impact upon us. We may come to feel that realism about the moral quality or meaning of life must go with accepting that living creatures are no more than genes, really only large molecules, and that all the manifestations of life must be explained in terms of the laws of matter. This, as we shall see, robs us of freedom and meaning.

There are, of course, those who protest against this effect of reductionism. For instance, biologist Paul A. Weiss, emeritus professor at Rockefeller University, New York, says at the end of an essay in the Alpbach Symposium, "The Living System: Determinism Stratified," *Beyond Reductionism* (ed. Koestler and Smythies, 1969): "organisms are not just heaps of molecules. At least, I cannot bring myself to feel like one, Can you?" He makes the broader point thus:

Biology has made spectacular advances by adopting the disciplined methods of the inorganic sciences and mathematics, but it has not widened its conceptual framework in equal measure . . . the need . . . may entail attempts in physics to enlarge its conceptual structure so as to be able not only to encompass living nature, but to fulfill the postulates raised by the realities of phenomena germane to living systems. (P. 42)

Biology thus is one discipline in which doubts have arisen about the reductionist assumption in scientific knowledge. If we attempt to reduce living creatures to the cause-and-effect explanations of physical science, the breaking down of their structure into component particles (or impulses, or whatever) means that certain manifestations that belong to the whole are lost sight of. And while perhaps with large molecules the laws of "energy requirements" or molecular attraction may be thought to explain what happens, when we come to even a very small living creature such as an amoeba, we observe *behavior:* the creature is capable of orienting self and *making choices*—and so we have to recognize another dimension in which it must be observed and contemplated. We may call the elements of this dimension its subjectivity, or its intentionality: it is a being, it operates from a center toward a world it perceives—by what some biologists call its "centricity." Somehow we must devise models of understanding capable of finding this reality.

And then, when we come to man, the question becomes far more complex and significant. Some concepts of man are absurd caricatures. Victor Frankl uncovers one (also in the Alpbach Symposium) where, according to an American text, man is "nothing but a complex biochemical mechanism powered by a combustion system which energises computers with prodigious storage facilities for retaining encoded information" (p. 403). But while we may smile at this, a similar "model" often appears in popular journals, and even in serious scientific thinking, as when analogies are made between "the brain" and a computer, showing cutaway diagrams of wires and terminals. Indeed, as Michael Polanyi has said,

Many scientists and philosophers have, for centuries now, asserted that all human beings, including themselves, are automatically functioning machines. (*Meaning*, p. 139)

As Gabriel Marcel declared, both because of the way he may be treated in society and because of this functional kind of philosophical view of existence, man may feel "submerged by his functions." This not only generates a view of human life that concentrates on the need to keep the functions in good order (an attitude often implicit in thinking about the sexual life, as in the Kinsey Reports), but it urges upon us a picture of life in which we have no volition, because we are no more than a collection of molecules operating according to the laws of physics and chemistry—so these must determine our behavior.

The predominance of this kind of scientific paradigm in our thinking has led to a situation in which science seems to have stripped the world of meaning.

To those of us who work in the humanities and especially education, this is a serious situation, even though many do not fully realize it. Yet, as we shall see, there have been those like Edmund Husserl who believe that we cannot go on living in such a world, and so believe that there is now a serious crisis in science itself. How shall we find a way out of this dilemma?

Let us return to philosophical anthropology. How shall we look at man? Man is an animal and is an object in the world because he has a body. But this body is so complex that, for one thing, it cannot be understood merely in terms of the reductionist paradigm. We need not suppose there to be anything "extra" to be added to man to distinguish him from the other animals. Yet there is a significant difference, which Martin Buber noted in *The Knowledge of Man* (p. 61). Animals live, as it were, like a fruit in its skin. They live and experience out of and into the center of their bodily lives. As Buber puts it, "An animal's 'image of the world,' or rather, its image of a realm, is nothing more than the dynamic of the presences bound up with one another by the functions of life which are to be carried out." Man's existence is different: for him a "world" exists. He is a "dweller in an enormous building which is always being added to, and whose limits he cannot penetrate, but which he can nevertheless know as one does know a house in which one lives." So, while we too live and experience out of the center of our bodily lives, our life out of this center has become reflective. We are "over against ourselves." We are able to contemplate ourselves, because as Marjorie Grene puts it, our life "sets itself to itself as its own." We are also capable of "grasping the whole building as such" we recognize that a world exists as an independent opposite from ourselves, and this is bound up with our capacity to recognize others as independent beings. Being, time, and space have a meaning and belong to experience in a different way for man.

Helmuth Plessner calls this man's "eccentric position." In man "the living thing is body, is in its body (as inner life) and outside the body as the point of view from which it is both (body and inner life)." The person is "subject of its experiences, of its perceptions and its actions, of its initiative. It knows and wills." As we grasp this special nature of man, we must come to see that this special kind of consciousness is bound up both with *relationship* and with *culture*. Our strange autonomous being, aware of past and future, and of place and other existences, could have been achieved only through a special kind of relationship—*being for*, largely with the mother in our formative infancy—and through the acquisition of the capacity to *symbolize*. As we shall see, philosophical anthropology relies very much on phenomenological disciplines, that is, disciplines that can examine the nature of consciousness, and these inevitably come to examine the kind of things symbolism and culture are, and how they emerge from the origins of being—which takes us into psychoanalytical discourse. Yet how these aspects of human existence are approached remains a problem; in Plessner's *Laughing and Crying,* for instance, he declares that his source is "just experience." As Marjorie Grene says in her foreword to this study, summarizing Plessner's mode of approach, "by this he means not only the abstract units of sense or feeling of traditional empiricism but simply everyday experience in the most ordinary and comprehensive sense."

> The sciences of man, poetry, painting, ordinary encounters of man with man; all this may be grist for the writer's mill (*Laughter and Crying,* p. xiii)

Wherever he can, he will garner insight into human nature. So, though this study of that "strange pair of human monopolies" is a classic in philosophical anthropology, it is difficult to place it "in any particular pigeonhole." All we can talk about is the "philosophical study of the nature of man."

Philosophical anthropology recognizes that in many areas of thought we are failing to make progress because there is something radically wrong with our paradigms in the humanities. We are especially susceptible to this problem in education, because this subject belongs, like English, to the humanities. Yet, in a scientific age, it may seem that the humanities are not dealing with realities. As Polanyi in *Meaning* puts it, "Science has most commonly been thought to deal with facts, the humanities with values. But since, in this frame of reference, values must be totally different from fact, the humanities have been thought to deal only with fancies." In the humanities, therefore, any attempt to establish meanings seems like an activity of the imagination, yielding works that are "brilliant in some cases, often sparkling and interesting, intriguing and enjoyable, but nevertheless inescapably only ephemeral flashes of light that never were—or could be—on sea or land" (p. 64). For this reason, we find, in many humanities subjects, individuals so fearful of seeming to be preoccupied with unrealities that they pin themselves down to some positivistic or "objective" study in the attempt to justify their existence.

Thus we find students in teacher training obliged to study, say, behaviorist and stimulus-response psychology which, they fully recognize, contributes little or nothing to their understanding of the children with whom they are working in teaching practice. On the other hand, books that look at the meaning of things to children, such as Len Chaloner's

Feeling and Perception in Young Children, and that would contribute enormously to their understanding are ignored. Or students training to be English teachers will be subjected to abstract exercises in linguistics, on the supposition that this will develop their capacity to deal with language in literature and in their pupils. "Research" is undertaken (say) into modes of experience, such as perception in infants, or the development of their capacity to talk. This research strives to be scientific and "objective" but it omits the very elements that to a phenomenologist would seem of primary importance, such as the meaning of gestures, intersubjectivity, and the loving presence of the mother in her function of "being for." Some summaries of research work in psychology have bravely admitted the paucity of results that much of this kind of science yields.[1]

The reason for this was indicated insightfully some time ago by Ernst Cassirer in *An Essay on Man.* Cassirer is a post-Kantian philosopher, concerned with Kant's fourth question, What is man? He declared that

> we cannot discover the nature of man in the same way that we can detect the nature of physical things. Physical things may be discussed in terms of their objective properties, but man may be described and defined only in terms of his consciousness . . . Empirical observation and logical analysis . . . here proved inefficient and inadequate. (*EM,* p. 5)

Cassirer's conclusion is that the key in understanding man is to recognize him as the *animal symbolicum:*

> Man has, as it were, discovered a new method of adapting himself to his environment. Between the receptor system and the effector system, which are found to be in all animal species, we find in man a third link which we may describe as the *symbolic system.* This new acquisition transforms the whole of human life. As compared with the other animals man lives not merely in a broader reality; he lives, so to speak, in a new *dimension* of reality. (*EM,* p. 24)

And this points very much to the aspects that Martin Buber was indicating above. Hence there follows a problem of how we seek to know this *animal symbolicum.* Cassirer says,

> it is only in our immediate intercourse with human beings that we have insight into the character of man. We must actually confront man, we must meet him squarely face to face, in order to understand him. (*EM,* p. 5)

But how? Cassirer opts for philosophical anthropology—or, rather, he calls it anthropological philosophy. And he urges us back to Socrates: "His philosophy—if he possesses a philosophy—is strictly anthropological." We need "a new activity and function of thought which is the distinctive feature of the philosophy of Socrates":

> only by way of dialogical or dialectic thought can we approach the knowledge of human nature.

And in this Cassirer seems to be trying to pick up a mode of discipline by which Greek philosophy sought to understand, but not in the empirical objective way. Truth may have come to be conceived as a sort of ready-made thing that could be grasped by an effort of the individual thinker. Cassirer asks for a concept of truth that is not that of an empirical object but is "the outgrowth of a social act." This means that we must think of our attempt to understand man in terms of that question "What is man?" but directed as seeing man as a creature who

> is constantly in search of himself—a creature who in every moment of his existence must examine and scrutinise the conditions of his existence. In this scrutiny, in this critical attitude to human life, consists the real value of human life. "A life which is unexamined," says Socrates in his *Apology,* "is not worth living" (Plato, *Apology* 37E Jowett trans.). . . . by this faculty of giving a response to himself and to others, . . . man becomes a "responsible" being, a moral subject. (*EM,* p. 6)

This is clearly an existentialist emphasis, and, as we shall see, the movement in philosophical anthropology contains the stream of existentialist philosophy. There are difficulties here, because fashionable thought is acquainted only with the more negative and nihilistic modes of existentialist thought. This kind of philosophy, however, began from the sense that to reduce man to the terms of "objective" science was, as Kierkegaard put it, a form of blasphemy, because it left everything out of account that makes us human: our unique experience, and our very capacity for examining our lives, and our "intentionality," our preoccupation with the future and with what we can bring into being. And here, as we shall see also, an important figure is Edmund Husserl.

Husserl believed, like Cassirer, that European science was in a state of crisis. He believed that there was an original impulse in Greek thought to pursue both truth in the objective world out there, and subjective truth, of the kind to which Cassirer refers. But gradually, and especially since the scientific revolution of the seventeenth century, thought had become too exclusively preoccupied with the "objective." The original impulse to explore all truth and experience, including subjective truth, was betrayed. And not only that: the positivistic concept of science in our time is, historically speaking, a *residual concept.* It has dropped all the questions that had been considered under the now narrower, now broader concepts of metaphysics, including all questions vaguely termed "ultimate and highest." Positivism, in a manner of speaking, decapitates philosophy. Even the ancient idea of philosophy, as unified in the indivisible unity of all being, implied a meaningful order of being and thus of problems of being. (Husserl, *Crisis*, p. 9).

Skepticism about the possibility of metaphysics, the collapse of the belief in a universal philosophy as the guide for the new man, actually, says Husserl, represents a collapse of the belief in "reason," "understood as the ancients opposed *epistēmē*— to *doxa.*"

> It is reason which ultimately gives meaning to everything that is thought to be, all things, values and ends,—their meaning understood as their normative relatedness to what, since the beginnings of philosophy, is meant by the word "truth." . . .
>
> If man loses this faith, it means nothing less than the loss of faith "in himself," in his own true being. (Ibid., pp. 12–13)

So, as will appear, we are concerned not only with more effective means of knowing ourselves and the world, but also with the question of whether the pursuit of truth is valid, and whether there can be *any meaning in life*. The prevalent feeling that life has no meaning is itself, as Michael Polanyi suggests, a consequence of the same doubtful paradigms behind our concepts of what thought is and of what can be known.

Philosophical anthropology may make use of any relevant discipline— psychology, neurophysiology, physical and social anthropology, sociology—but it *is* none of these, and its perspective does not belong to any one philosophical school.

At the same time it represents an attempt to return to *the problem of life*. In philosophy as established in our intellectual traditions there has been an attempt in this century to dismiss metaphysics and the philosophy of being. The predominant schools have concerned themselves with logic and verification, and anything that has no findable referent belongs to nonproblems and nonstatements. Yet, as E. W. F. Tomlin has argued, the problems that the philosopher dodges return to plague him, and his vocation must be to attempt to "interpret the universe," willy-nilly. He is professionally obliged to inquire into the meaning and value of life. Even where philosophers have renounced any such obligation, and have attempted a determined avoidance of metaphysics, they have displayed a tacit metaphysic of their own: in combating dogma the positivists have adopted a dogmatic manner quite as formidable as that of their traditional adversaries (*EP*, p. 308). There are those who find a certain bankruptcy in analytical philosophy (e.g., Marjorie Grene herself, Roger Poole, and Tomlin). They find that its air of problem-solving is really a technique of problem-dodging, not least at times by reducing everything to problems of language.

In philosophical anthropology we have the attempt at least to confront the problem of a philosophy of being, and to tackle the real problems of life. Perhaps this is the moment to tabulate some of the component disciplines. I have already indicated some of the movements that have contributed to the new discipline. There is the *post-Kantian* philosophy of Ernst Cassirer and Susanne Langer. There is the *postcritical* philosophy of Michael Polanyi and Marjorie Grene. There is Martin Buber's particular kind of philosophical anthropology and the phenomenological critique of the nature of knowledge made by Edmund Husserl.

Below I shall try to relate all these disciplines historically. The main philosophical movement that has tried to deal with man and his experience in a whole way, fully embracing his subjectivity, has been *existentialism*. But here we shall have to make many qualifications, because up to now existentialism too has been assumed to be a very somber and pessimistic philosophy that dwells (as in Sartre) on the futility of human existence and the triumph of nothingness. I call this, with no great accuracy, the "old" existentialism. In this book I want to lead on to the *new existentialism*, and we shall have to work quite hard to see how it moves on from the "old" existentialism which, although it began by trying, in the name of the human spirit to challenge the predominance of the scientific, functional view of man, found itself unable to find its way out of a nihilistic impasse as frustrating and blank as the philosophies it set out to oppose.

The new existentialism is bound up with *phenomenology*—a philosophical discipline that pays attention to the study of the *phenomena of consciousness,* employing subjective disciplines that attend to *meaning,* problems of perception, and learning.[2]

The terms are often forbidding (we may talk, for example, of *phenomenological existentialism*) and these disciplines have their own jargon.[3] Some books that are important in the movement are almost unreadable for a lay person (such as Edmund Husserl's *Ideas* and Merleau-Ponty's *Phenomenology of Perception.*) But the heart of the whole movement is sound, and the complexities of language and argument arise from the daunting nature of the struggle to grasp the very complexities that this movement has decided to face in our everyday existence. For there are enormous problems that it is trying to open up, even in ordinary everyday seeing and hearing, in perceiving our world and acting in it, not to speak of our relationship with other people and with ourselves, our inner fantasies, and our bodies. One of the excitements of the new movement is that it demolishes many of the old simplistic theories, of how we see and sense; how "the brain" "works" and how behavior may be explained in mechanistic terms,[4] or how the analysis of molecular structures and dynamics can account for life.

On the other hand, it offers us more than mere dry intellectual systems, for the emphasis in existentialism is on self-realization—on finding new capacities in ourselves, a new sense of our creativity, of our capacities for vision. Philosophical anthropology offers new opportunities for us to find "authenticity" and freedom, as well as new responsibilities, for one central emphasis, as we shall see, is that knowing is an ethical act, involving the whole person.

Thus our quest is not merely a quest for knowledge for its own sake; knowledge brings responsibilities and moral obligations, bound up with central questions of human freedom and survival. This is the new emphasis found in existentialism, postcritical philosophy, and phenomenology. Something has been wrong with our concept of knowledge and this has led to serious problems in our approach to the world and ourselves, problems whose roots may even be said to be pathological.[5]

Obviously, all these problems—of self-fulfillment, of our moral stance toward the world, and of our notion of ourselves—are of profound concern in psychotherapy, so that here we need to invoke various schools of psychoanalysis as spheres of nourishment in philosophical anthropology.

In his book *In Search of Philosophical Understanding*, E. A. Burtt grasps the nettle firmly:

> The most provocative note in the findings I want to share is the conviction that philosophy must come fully to terms with the psychoanalytic concept of the human mind. (P. xiv)

Psychoanalysis opens up a whole sphere of human truth. In Greek thought truth was basically a theory of *being*,[6] during modern times it has been mainly a quest for *method*. In discussing existentialism, Burtt considers how philosophy comes again to explore the nature of being and is seeking to use the disastrous split between "science" and philosophy as the exploration of the whole truth of man.[7]

Our key to understanding in this realm of being is the experience of intersubjectivity—encounter, relationship, and love—and this is a central theme in both psychoanalysis and existentialist philosophy of the "new" kind. The central insight of religious existentialism (as Burtt says) is a search for love. As a child, man's consuming need is to be loved, so that he can find his way from anxiety, frustration, and anger in the presence of the harsh realities that surround him, to an acceptance of his adult role in the universe.

How is this body of understanding in psychoanalysis constituted? Why should we take any notice of psychoanalytical theory? The answer is that it offers a phenomenological discipline: it has to do with the meanings of consciousness, whatever "school" we take. And it represents an empirical discipline of a special kind.

D. W. Winnicott makes a useful list of the psychoanalyst's and pediatri-

cian's sources of understanding of human nature (his own in fact) in his
essay "Paediatrics and Psychiatry" in *Collected Papers:*
1. Through direct observation of the infant-mother relationship.
2. Direct periodical observation of an infant starting soon after birth
   and continuing over a period of years.
3. Paediatric history-taking ("in my own experience I have given a
   mother the opportunity of telling me what she knows of her infant's
   development in about 20,000 cases").
4. Paediatric practice typically the management of infant feeding and
   excretion.
5. Diagnostic interview with the child.
6. Actual psychoanalytical experience. ("This gives a different view
   of the patient's infancy according to whether the child is in the 2-4
   year-old age group, or older, or near puberty, or in adolescence.
   For the analyst who is doing research on the earliest processes of
   emotional development, the analysis of fairly normal adults can
   even be more profitable than the analysis of children!")
7. The observation in paediatric practice of psychotic regressions
   appearing as they commonly do in childhood or even in infancy.
8. Observation of children in homes adapted to cope with difficulties,
   whether these are antisocial behaviour, confessional states, mani-
   acal episodes, relationships distorted by suspicion, or persecution,
   or mental defect, or fits.
9. The psychoanalysis of schizophrenics. (*CP*, pp. 158–59)

The sources of psychoanalytical insight, in other words, lie in the
experience of patients whose problems are illuminated by subjective disciplines, which begin to allow us to understand their experience, and their
needs, through the study of the meanings of consciousness.

Therefore, in seeking to pursue the new perspectives offered to philosophy and psychology by the new subjective disciplines, there are many
points at which a student might begin. A person with a political and
philosophical bent might start with Roger Poole's *Towards Deep Subjectivity.* Someone interested in literature and especially in William Blake
might begin with Theodore Roszak's *Where The Wasteland Ends* or F. R.
Leavis's *The Living Principle.* Scientists interested in the philosophy of
science might try Marjorie Grene's *Approaches to a Philosophical Biology* or *The Understanding of Nature.* Psychologists might try Liam Hud-
son, *The Cult of the Fact,* or Erwin Straus, *Phenomenological
Psychology,* or Alan Gould and John Shotter, *Human Action and Its
Psychological Investigations.*

Those interested in psychiatry could begin with Jan Foudraine, *Not
Made of Wood,* or Peter Lomas, *True and False Experience.* Sociologists
could begin with the work of John O'Neill, such as his *Essaying Mon-
taigne.* Karl Stern in *The Flight from Woman* discusses thought in philosophy in relation to gender.

But whatever our starting point, we need to put up signposts as we go—not least because the whole development of this new holistic approach to man and his world, so different from that of our strict positivism and natural scientism, has been widely ignored so far. This is, I believe, partly due to historical circumstances—two wars against Germany, with a consequent neglect of German thought, have no doubt contributed. In America the influence of German philosophy has, on the other hand, been conveyed by the movement of refugees from Nazism. But the domination of philosophical thought by Newton, Locke, Hume, and (in recent times) by Russell and the logical positivists still holds established approaches in a paradigm that is essentially hostile to the Continental (Leibnitzian) tradition, that of "reflective" philosophy. Our way of thinking is imbued with a model of the mind that sees it as the passive recipient of impressions or "stumuli," so that the way to understand it is by microanalysis of events or mechanisms, in atomistic terms. The Leibnitzian or "Continental" view sees the mind as more active in perception, and as to be understood by participation, as in phenomenology: it requires the *Geisteswissenschaften*, and the disciplines implied by the words *hermeneutics*, the science of methodological interpretation, and *ontology*, the science of being.

In British thought one significant figure would have understood this: Samuel Taylor Coleridge. He persisted in seeking a view of the mind that found its creative participation in the perception of reality. Recognition of his explorations here is long overdue. F. R. Leavis, for example, was singularly unfair to Coleridge.

One major problem, however, is that we still have fully to define *phenomenology*. Herbert Spiegelberg's masterly surveys, on which much of what I write here is based, are primarily concerned with phenomenology, though he also discusses psychoanalytical theory. But he does not often discuss those more interesting applications of this kind of approach, such as, for example, Winnicott's work, which is in a sense phenomenology in practice. As Roger Poole says in his account of Husserl's work, "There exists no study, as far as I know which is genuinely comprehensible to the layman."[8] This is hardly surprising, he adds, because Husserl had great difficulty himself in expressing what he meant, which he also changed and developed from year to year. Poole also says that there is no definitive account of phenomenology, no general agreement on terms, nor could there ever be. It is a subject in development, everyone making of it what he will for his own work (while possibly the best manifestations of this discipline are in its applications in criticism).

Even in psychotherapy progress is slow, as Spiegelberg admits:

one must be under no illusions; the present role of phenomenology in the total picture of psychology and psychiatry, particularly in the Anglo-

American world, is a minor one and has not shown significant growth in recent years except at the "fringes." . . . Its academic influence in the major universities and departments is likewise unimpressive (*Phenomenology in Psychology and Psychiatry*, p. 364)

Gilbert Ryle, who in 1949 wrote *The Concept of Mind*, embraced German phenomenological philosophy in the twenties, but then turned against it. And while he renounced a reductionist position, he did not solve the problem of mind, though he did at least see that the Newtonian system was not the only paradigm in natural science, and even spoke of "my phenomenology of mind."[9]

Spiegelberg suggests that while Husserl may be a new interest within British philosophy, his work has had little or no effect on British empirical psychology. This is a serious problem for education, and a sad aspect of British intellectual life.

The one dominant figure in English analytical philosophy, Ludwig Wittgenstein, ignored phenomenology, though some believe there may be a kind of rapprochement between his later philosophy and descriptive phenomenology.

The problem is not one of difficulties of language or tranlation. There are clearly metaphysical and paradigmatic obstacles. Merleau-Ponty, Erwin Straus, and the phenomenologists, even Sartre in his perverse way, confront the living mystery in the body, love, being, and death. As Roger Poole puts it, [he must recognize] "the fact that we exist in bodies of flesh and blood, and the fact that we think in loops of intellection which vanish the moment they are thought." The British philosophical tradition shrinks from such *embodiment*, and so we are faced with a very complex and taxing situation in trying to obtain for these disciplines proper attention.

What we must do, in education and the humanities, is to insist that there are, as we know from literature and music, real problems of being, which we have a right to tackle, and for this purpose, to use Roger Poole's phrase, we must claim our right to a "philosophical space." It is appropriate for every man to ponder the meaning of existence, and it is right and necessary for philosophy to tackle such questions as What is man? Does our life have a meaning? Is there a God? How did life come into existence? How did consciousness come into being? What values can be derived from our knowledge of man and the world?

To shirk the issues of the philosophy of being is a betrayal (as Husserl declared) of the original telos of philosophy in our civilization, in the pursuit of truth in ancient Greek thought, and in its impulse to investigate both inner and outer reality.

For philosophy to find what Marcel calls an "echo in our lives" depends on the way in which philosophy is situated in relation to truth.[10] Philosophy, in resisting the dehumanization of our time, must accept that, however tainted with "subjectivity" it may be, thought can remain alive only if it embodies an idea of man and of human values (Marcel, *Tragic Wisdom,* p. 30). There is a great deal to do, as Marjorie Grene shows us, in studying the nature of man, and evolution, the unfolding of the multifarious forms of nature, and the apparent development of higher levels of being. What is man's role in life and being? Spiegelberg quotes, in his essay on Binswanger, a motto from Kierkegaard: "Above all, let us hold fast on to what it means to be a man" *(Concluding Unscientific Postscript).* In all our difficulties of indicating and defining the new perspectives in philosophy and psychology, that ought to provide our main bearing.

Notes

1. See, for instance, on the failure of empirical psychology, a review of work on "Memory and Verbal Learning" in the *Annual Review of Psychology,* 1970, by Tulving and Madigan. Also see *Training Tomorrow's Psychiatrists* by Marshall Edelson and Theodore Lidz, who write, "We are witness to the bankruptcy of positivism as a sufficient frame of reference for the behavioural scientist." They try to explore the possibility of basing a system of training on Ernst Cassirer's philosophy.

On alternative methods for studying the nature of human experience see Roger Poole, *Towards Deep Subjectivity* (London: Allen Lane, 1972); the work of Aaron Esterson and R. D. Laing; and the latter's *Interpersonal Perception: A Theory and a Method of Research,* with H. Phillipson and A. R. Lee (New York: Springer, 1960).

2. Not, of course, to be confused with *phenomenalism,* which is the view that human knowledge is coupled to phenomena and can never attain to the real nature of things.

3. There are also problems of the vagaries of fashion. Asked whether he accepted the label *Christian existentialist* by his publisher, Gabriel Marcel made a concession. "But very soon when I became aware of the inanities the word 'existentialism' led to, and especially among society women, I was sorry to have been so accommodating." *Tragic Wisdom and Beyond* (Evanston, Ill.: Northwestern University Press, 1973), p. 238.

4. See Jan Foudraine on the determination in medicine to reduce life-problems to an organic cause, in the tradition of E. Kraepelin, in *Not Made of Wood* (New York: Macmillan, 1974), pp. 9ff. See also his chaps. 16 and 17.

5. See Karl Stern, *The Flight from Woman* (London: Unwin, 1970).

6. As E. R. Dodds says in *The Greeks and the Irrational* (Berkeley: University of California Press, 1959), "Man . . . enjoys in daily alternation two distinct kinds of experience—ὕπαρ and ὄναρ as the Greeks called them . . . and he has no obvious reason for thinking one of them more significant than the other . . ." (p. 102).

7. Here a useful book is E. W. F. Tomlin, *Living and Knowing* (London: Faber and Faber, 1955).

8. Poole, *Towards Deep Subjectivity,* p. 78.

9. See D. C. S. Osterhuizen, "Phenomenological Psychology," *Mind* 79 (1968): 487–501, which relates Ryle to Husserl.

10. Grene quotes E. A. Burtt, "Descriptive Metaphysics," *Mind* (1963): 18–39. Burtt's *In Search of Philosophic Understanding* is again of great importance here.

2
Toward a More Whole View of Man

The kind of emphasis on wholeness that philosophical anthropology is making is not new. Charles Dickens and D. H. Lawrence, William Blake and the Romantic Poets, for example, have been among those in literature who have resisted the reduction of man in his own thinking to a mechanism, or have upheld the claims of unique being against quantitative or utilitarian approaches. F. R. Leavis invoked such writers against what he called the "technologico-Benthamite calculus."[1] So let me try to make it easier for the literary reader, who comes to the problem from the arts and humanities, to see the connection between the issues in philosophy and creative art.

There is a superb passage in D. H. Lawrence's novel *Kangaroo* in which he shows himself aware of the problem:

The study of collective psychology to-day is absurd in its inadequacy. Man is supposed to be an automaton working in certain automatic ways when you touch certain springs. These springs are all labelled: they form a keyboard to the human psyche, according to modern psychology. And the chief labels are hard instinct, collective interest, hunger, fear, collective prestige, and so on.

But the only way to make any study of collective psychology is to study the isolated individual. Upon your conception of the single individuals, all your descriptions will be based, all your sciences established. For this reason the human sciences, philosophy, ethics, psychology, politics, economics, can never be sciences at all. There can never be an exact science dealing with individual life. *L'anatomia presuppone il cadavere:* anatomy presupposes a corpse, says D'Annunzio. You can establish an exact science on a corpse, supposing you start with the corpse, and don't try to derive it from a living creature. But upon life itself, or any instance of life, you cannot establish a science.

Because even science must start from definition, or from precise description. And you can never define or precisely describe any living creature. Iron must remain iron, or cease to exist. But a rabbit might evolve into something which is still rabbit, and yet different from that which a rabbit now is. So how can you define or precisely describe a rabbit? There is always the unstable *creative* element present in life, and this science can never tackle. Science is cause-and-effect.

Before we can begin any of the so-called humane sciences we must take on trust a purely unscientific fact: namely, that every living creature has an individual soul, however trivial or rudimentary, which connects it individually with the source of all life, as man, in the religious terminology, is connected with God, and inseparable from God. To call this connection the will-to-live is not quite sufficient. It is more than a will-to-persist. It is a will-to-live in the further sense, a will-to-change, a will-to-evolve, a will towards further creation of the self. The urge towards evolution if you like. But it is more than evolution. There is no simple cause-and-effect sequence. The change from caterpillar to butterfly is not cause and effect. It is a new gesture in creation. Science can wriggle as hard as it likes, but the change from caterpillar to butterfly is utterly unscientific, illogical, and *unnatural,* if we take science's definition of nature. It is an answer to the strange creative urge, the God-whisper, which is the one and only everlasting motive for everything.

So then man. He is said to be a creature of cause-and-effect, or a creature of free-will. The two are the same. Free-will means acting according to reasoned choice, which is a purest instance of cause-and-effect. Logic is the quintessence of cause-and-effect. And idealism, the ruling of life by the instrumentality of the idea, is precisely the mechanical, even automatic cause-and-effect process. The idea, or ideal, becomes a fixed principle, and life, like any other force, is driven into mechanical repetition of given motions—millions of times over and over again—according to the fixed ideal. (Heinemann ed., pp. 330–31)

There are may valuable insistences here. But the air of "thinking aloud" in the passage points to our problem. Lawrence is groping toward the recognition of being, and the dimension of intentionality, but his insights are not, and could not at that time be, adequately organized to serve as an answer to the questions raised. Lawrence rightly insisted on the need to "study the isolated individual," but yet the word *isolated* is not right, nor does he say how the individual can properly be studied. He sees that "objective" study tends to belong to a mode of thinking that explores a universe of dead objects, and that studies of man have not yet learned to study man as a living and developing being. But he does not endeavor to disentangle the philosophical arguments around this problem. He insists upon the need to take account of the developing creative urge in all natural life, of which man is a part, and so emphasizes the aspect of man with which the existentialists have become preoccupied. Lawrence points, in his characteristically untidy way, to differences between modes of thought. He sees the reductionist effect of deterministic mechanical attitudes to "cause and effect" in accounts of human makeup, and its implicit threat to being and freedom. But Lawrence was writing a novel, at a great pace. He simply throws out his asides and leaves them. So while he held his banner high, inscribed "God-whisper!" he does no more than oblige us to begin to see that there are problems lurking in the mistaken explanations of the "exact sciences," especially when they are applied to life and especially human life. We may link this passage with the experiences of Ursula Brangwen in *The Rainbow*. No doubt in this Lawrence is recording something of his own experience at college. It is a common kind of disillusionment: the student often finds that his college or university has not provided the excitement, the illumination, for which he has hoped. In this respect, matters have not changed sufficiently, and the underlying reason, I believe, is a philosophical one.[2]

As the reader will remember, Ursula Brangwen in *The Rainbow* approaches her teacher training college with awe: "She wanted all the students to have a high, pure spirit. She wanted them to say only the real, genuine things. . . ." In the college buildings themselves, she sees "a reminiscence of the wondrous, cloistral origin of education." But then, after a few weeks, "college was barren, cheap, a temple converted to the most vulgar, petty commerce. Had she not gone to hear the echo of learning pulsing back to the source of the mystery?" And in her botany laboratory, the mystery still glimmers, even as she feels she is degrading herself, because the professors only offered her "ready-made stuff." The account of a young student's feelings is still valid, where the "staff" have still not made the connection between the mystery and the theory, between the existential reality of the young student, who is perceiving the world with fresh vision, and the theoretical account of existence that he or she is taught. Lawrence brings out the contrast with one of his vivid moments, an existential moment, like that in an Impressionist painting:

> A sort of inertia came over her. Mechanically, from habit, she went on with her studies. But it was almost hopeless. She could scarcely attend to anything . . . she sat looking down, out of the window, hearing no word. . . . Down below, in the street, the sunny grey pavement went beside the palisade. A woman in a pink frock, with a scarlet sunshade, crossed the road, a little white dog running like a fleck of light about her. The woman with the scarlet sunshade came over the road, a lilt in her walk, a little shadow attending her. Ursula watched her spellbound. The woman with the scarlet sunshade and the flickering terrier was gone— and whither? Whither?
>
> In what world of reality was the woman in the pink dress walking? To what warehouse of dead unreality was she herself confined? . . . What good was this place, this college? . . . when one only learned . . . in order to answer examination questions, in order that one should have a higher commercial value later on? (*The Rainbow* Penguin ed., 1973, p. 435)

Life outside moves in an unfolding free movement of creative time: we have a glimpse of a creature, a being, moving along with a living aura like Manet's *Femme à l'Ombrelle*. The dry intellectual material of "Education," absorbed for exams, seems, by contrast, dead. Ursula Brangwen's problem is that of relating "science" as part of knowledge to one's relationship with the world—and one's personal life. Lawrence depicts his heroine brooding as a student on this question while she is studying biology. One of her lecturers, a woman doctor of physics, represents the mechanistic scientific view:

> "No, really," Dr. Frankstone had said, "I don't see why you should attribute some special mystery to life—do you? We don't understand it as we understand electricity, even, but that doesn't warrant our saying it is something special, something different in kind and distinct from everything else in the universe—do you think it does? May it not be that life consists in a complexity of physical and chemical activities, of the same order as the activities we already know in science? I don't see, really, why we should imagine there is a special order of life, and life alone." (Ibid., p. 440)

Dr. Frankstone's may be taken to represent that reductive view, which can fallaciously extend itself thus into a general philosophy—a positivist metaphysic. When this scientist speaks of "chemical and physical activities" she really means ways of describing such aspects of reality as are capable of being described in such terms, in one dimension or "projection" merely. She forgets that is not the whole of the matter: much of the secret of life still escapes us. Reductionism is a method of science—a quite legitimate one for its purposes—which approaches living things as no more than "agglomerations of molecules." But insofar as it tends to see them as *nothing but* physico-chemical substances, and no more than interlocking mechanisms, it becomes fallacious, and bad science.

Science as generally taught implies to students that things simply *are,* and have come into being by chance and necessity: the universe is simply a vast machine. But what about mind? Consciousness, if it is recognized at all, has come into the picture by some miraculous jump from a purely physico-chemical complex to the sphere of "mind." Few scientists realize how obscurantist this belief is, and what irrational assumptions it involves. We urgently need a new kind of philosophy of science, to make it possible to see a continuity throughout nature, from the activities of matter in inorganic substance, through lower forms of life to the higher, and on to man. As Tomlin points out, many scientists and those who follow scientific thought suggest that consciousness is a product of "the brain," or "the nervous system." Yet it is clear that forms of life without either brain or nervous system operate with autonomy. The amoeba, for example, breathes, responds to stimuli, moves about, avoids objects, and reproduces, without either brain or nervous system. It must be regarded as a subject—it relates from a center to an environment and has "centricity"—

a kind of freedom in the world. It may not have "consciousness," but it has a centricity without a brain, so in what does this faculty reside? All we can say is in "life," indicating a quality we recognize that is not a sum of the physical or chemical components, but is a manifestation of complex beings.

As Marjorie Grene argues, here are serious shortcomings in the prevalent scientific view because science in our traditions has proved unable to find "the category of life." "Objective" science tends to impress upon us the belief that all the "objective" is "real": the object, says Tomlin, seemed to have a monopoly of reality. What then about the consciousness of the scientist, or anyone else, *knowing* the reality? This indeed is a problem, but most scientists simply adhere to the faith that, ultimately, this will be explained in physico-chemical terms. So too will the origin of life, development, and all the dynamics of biological forms. Life will ultimately be created in the laboratory. The autonomy of biology will be undermined at the molecular level, and all biological processes will be explicable in terms of quantum mechanics. The biologists are at last getting down to basic facts: "from every point of view biology is getting nearer and nearer to the molecular level," as F. H. Crick put it in *The Scientific American* (September 1957).

But, as Polanyi points out, these are all checks overdrawn on some future bank account. The ultimate connections and explanations have never been made. And Polanyi declares that they never could be: reductive explanations could never, because of their very nature, explain the secrets of life that they so confidently explain away.

The effect of such problems on one's philosophy of life was clear to D. H. Lawrence. In *The Rainbow* Ursula puzzles over whether she herself is a mere agglomeration of "forces" such as science describes, or whether there is some other dynamic in life to which she belongs:

But the purpose, what was the purpose? Electricity had no soul, light and heat had no soul. Was she herself an impersonal force, or conjunction of forces, like one of these?

She is looking at a plant-animal under the microscope:

She looked still at the unicellular shadow that lay within the field of light, under her microscope. *It was alive—she saw the bright mist of its ciliary activity, she saw the gleam of its nucleus,* as it slid across the plane of light. What then was its will? It was a conjunction of forces, physical and chemical, what held these forces unified, and for what purposes were they unified?
  For what purpose were the incalculable physical and chemical activities nodalized in this shadowy, moving speck under her microscope?

What was the will which nodalized them and created the one thing she saw? What was its intention? To be itself? Was its purpose just mechanical and limited to itself?

It intended to be itself. But what self? Suddenly in her mind the world gleamed strangely, with an intense light, like the nucleus of the creature under the microscope. Suddenly she had passed away into an intensely-gleaming light of knowledge. She could not understand what it all was. She only knew that it was not limited mechanical energy, nor mere purpose of self-preservation and self-assertion. It was a consummation, a being infinite. Self was at oneness with the infinite. To be oneself was a supreme, gleaming triumph of identity. (Ibid., pp. 440–41, emphasis added)

Inspired by such philosophical thoughts about "life," Ursula tries to find and to realize herself. Her impulse takes the path of a love affair with Skrebensky, which turns out, in the end to be no fulfillment.

For present purposes, the passage from Lawrence's novel communicates two significant things. One is that we are very much influenced in our personal choices and living conduct, by the concept we hold of ourselves; and this in turn is much affected by the implicit metaphysics of science. Ursula is shown to be struggling with the concept of living existence held by the physics lecturer—that there need by "no mystery" is our attitudes to life, and that everything is really to be described and regarded in terms of the sum of its mechanical qualities and processes. The limited "scientific" descriptions of reality in reductionism has been extended by this scientific teacher to human existence, and has become a false extension of scientific methodology into a general philosophy of life. Ursula intuitively feels that she must rebel and flies into the arms of her lover, to find the sphere of "being." Yet her pursuit is too willfully intellectual, even there; she has not yet learned to be.

Fortunately, Ursula has her author to rescue her from nihilism. Lawrence is also able to communicate how the scientific discipline itself can bring awe, and a deep sense of wonder and mystery, as many scientists admit. True science, he knew, can be in this way an important cultural activity, not only bringing a respect for truth and for the mysterious complexity of existence, but also enabling an individual to ponder and develop a meaningful sense of his own being, his own existence in the cosmos. Here, pondering the existence and nature of a small creature gives Ursula a sense of how she must fulfill her own being in the human sphere in a different way. This enables her to find a sense of relationship between her separate existence, and her union with all created life. Lawrence sees that there is a continuity from primary consciousness to the highly developed consciousness of the adult human woman, with her need for meaning, to be worked on through symbolism and culture in relation to her experience of intersubjectivity.

In discussing the implications of Lawrence's treatment of Ursula and science in *The Rainbow* I have considered many concepts that would be viewed by the positivist or the academic philosopher as not really "real," because they cannot be subjected to scientific investigation or "validation" in the "objective" paradigm. They have to do also with those metaphysical questions about being, love, and the meaning of life, which the logical positivist dismisses as "emotional" nonsense, and which many a university philosophy department abjures ("Ah! Nonphilosophy!"). Yet, as Lawrence's novel shows, these issues can be central to a young person's life, and Ursula cannot go on living unless she struggles with them, trying to solve very real problems of living.

Students respond with understanding and enthusiasm to these issues as evoked in a novel like *The Rainbow*. They recognize them as real problems that they themselves have encountered, and can see how they relate to Ursula's experience of education, both as a student and as a teacher. Even as student teachers are taught a psychology and a philosophy that often fail to illuminate anything they do, they will gladly bring to bear on their practical work and living the kind of issues Lawrence raises in his novel.

If we follow the lead of philosophers like E. A. Burtt and include in our approach the findings of psychoanalysis, then we shall need to recognize problems like Ursula's as real. The established perspectives that attach themselves to scientific objectivity can never find many of the problems with which the novelist deals: the yearnings of "being," unconscious motives, body-meaning—these can only be found by "subjective" disciplines. So what is called for is nothing less than a complete revision of our attitudes to human nature and the way we conduct discourse and study about it.

Perhaps we already call some of the dimensions "Lawrentian"—uncanny and mysterious aspects of the human self and its potentialities, very much bound up with the processes of learning such as Ursula is shown experiencing. Marjorie Grene uses terms such as *transcendence* and *immanence,* following existentialism, for example. Many therapists speak of inarticulate communication between themselves and patients, as through "body meanings" or facial expressions. Lawrence shows himself well aware of the ineffable areas of experience, and places before us the problem of how to examine and understand these modes, which are certainly found in teaching, as Lawrence's poems about that experience show.[3] How can we explore the relationship between intersubjectivity and perception, in relation to what Leavis called "the living principle"?

We only have to consider one simple ability—that of recognizing a face—to show the complexities of "knowing." In Polanyi we find some useful terms to come at the ineffable, like *subception* and *indwelling.* Grene summarizes Polanyi's examination of the problem thus:

The *objective transcendence* of my recognition (of a face, etc.) to use Szilasi's term, its other-directedness, is at one with what we may call its *subjective immanence,* the foundation, assimilated to myself, upon which it rests. This analysis Polanyi has recently elaborated in reliance on psychological experiments on "subception," which seem to confirm the significance of subsidiary factors in perceptual behaviour. In philosophical terms, one could equally take the recognition of physiognomies in Polanyi's account of it as illustrating the existentialist thesis that our being is *being in a world.* My awareness is not separate subject "in-itself" but at one and the same time an assimilation of what is beyond and an extension of myself into the thing beyond. (*KK,* p. 56)

In this kind of philosophical anthropology we have highly acute minds requiring attention to the poetic, the inward, the symbolizing faculty of man, and this should make for approaches to psychology and philosophy that are more recognizably relevant to the experience of teaching, as well as more meaningful in the humanities.

There is no mysticism or animism or even religious content in this opening up of new realities and modes of awareness (and it can be given assent to by both agnostic and believer). It is the kind of awed recognition that asserts, as does psychologist M. O'C. Drury, that all understanding of life is a question of mystery:

I want to make "wonder secure." There is a danger, with the ever increasing development of natural science, its powerful applications, and its inevitable specialisation, that we come to forget the realm of the inexplicable. "The mysteriousness of our present being." (*Danger,* p. 77)

Again, it is not a question of "two cultures," but rather one of recognizing that learning is a process involving the whole being. The many complaints made by students that their experience of a university or college, like Ursula's, has not been a rich one, or even a satisfactory one, perhaps reveals a failure to recognize this wholeness in the learning process. Where education has proved arid, there are perhaps two failures. One had to do with a shrinking from the kind of close relationship that is essential if there is to be whole development. The other may be that of failing to conceive of education as a process involving commitment and responsibility, that is, to see that learning is bound up with values and existential choice and action, and demands the inevitable confrontation with living issues.

There is a need to heal the "dissociation of sensibility" by bringing together the two forms of knowing. Marjorie Grene emphasizes the subtle web and dynamic of our life-world and how we must continually attend to *both* our world of primary experience and the intellectual and cultural world.

She goes on to make it plain that when the biologist Adolf Portmann speaks of this need for unity, he is talking about the areas of experience to which the psychoanalysts are pointing, together with the post-Kantian philosophers, phenomenologists, and "new" existentialists. In Portmann we have a *scientist* emphasizing that the *life-world* in which we live is bound up with *imagination* and *vision* (and that we cannot have reason and science without these):

> The world in which, from infancy, we come to live, and the human world shared by members of all cultures, does of course, include the surface of experience, the colours, the sounds, the rhythms of movement that confront us on all sides. But it includes also our feelings, our desires, our dreams, the creative aspirations of artists, the vision of saints and prophets, even the delusions of the insane. No single terms can adequately characterise this whole range of primary experience; perhaps we can still speak here of the "life world" if we remember that it is more than the plain, open order of "common sense" to which we are referring. Such a life world, then, with all its opacities and ambiguities, stands in contrast with the limited but lucid sphere governed by the operations of the intellect—and that means, in our culture, by the operation of science and technology. Human nature comprises both and can dispense with neither. (*AB*, p. 50)

How useful to have this emphasis from a philosopher of science discussing a European biologist, and pointing to the at-one-ness of science and technology with the imaginative and creative powers!

The first step in our approach to the problem of philosophy and psychology in the humanities then is to see that what is inevitably involved is a biological philosophy, including a completely new notion of man's place in nature. Moreover, we cannot progress until we accept that we need a new model of man arising from this. Marjorie Grene raises the question over Helmuth Plessner, the philosophical biologist:

> There can be no resolution of the problem of the *Geisteswissenschaften* ["study of how the spirit knows"], Plessner declares, without a general philosophy of man, "philosophical anthropology." But a philosophical anthropology is in turn impossible, he says, unless it is itself founded on philosophy of nature . . . in the sense of a philosophical examination of the question *What it means to be alive*. (*AB*, p. 65)

This kind of philosophical biology is trying to devise a new way of understanding living creatures, and when it comes to man finds additional dimensions, such as his culture, and all those manifestations which develop out of "encounter," that is, out of love. These are *biological* facts, but of course not facts such as would recommend themselves to the strict positivist. Biology, however, has itself found the primacy of love as the source of being, social life, and culture. From the study of organic forms in life it progresses to discover specifically human attributes and sees how our cultural dimensions is a natural development from our biological form. A positivist biology has never been able to find "full human nature":

> What is "full human nature"? Portmann has mentioned its three chief characters; upright posture, speech, and rational action. Now, all these have to be *learned* by the infant in its first months through contact with human adults or in particular with one adult, his mother or foster mother. Of course parental care, and life in general, are essential, in a host of intricate and marvellous ways, to a host of other species as well. But nowhere else in living nature on this planet does this pattern of premature sociality occur. (*AB,* p. 47)

This unique period of postembryonic, yet still embryonic, growth is called by Adolf Portmann the period of *social gestation.* It demands not only nine months in the uterus, but a further twelve months in the "social uterus of maternal care." It is like that psychic parturition with which psychoanalysis concerns itself, not least because this is a dynamic that involves the creative imagination and other intuitive capacities on the mother's part, and in the emerging infant's capacity to become himself according to "the formative principle" in his living processes.

As Marjorie Grene insists, following Portmann, this development of cultural dynanmics in man is no "afterthought": it is a central reality of our very existence, the special quality of man.

> . . . Our unique pattern of development is not an "afterthought" tacked on to a standard embryogenesis. The human attitudes and endowments which we must acquire in infancy are prepared for very early in embryonic growth: thus the first preparation for the upright posture, in the development of the pelvis, occurs in the second month of the foetus's growth. The preparation for the acquisition of speech, moreover, involves glottal structures very strikingly and thoroughly different from those of any other species. And the huge size of our infants relatively to the young of apes—born more "mature" but very much smaller—is probably related, Portmann conjectures, to the immense development of the brain necessary for the achievement of human rationality—a development which begins, again, very early indeed in ontogenesis. In short, the whole biological development of a typical mammal *has been rewritten in our case in a new key:* the whole structure of the embryo, the whole rhythm of growth is directed, from first to last, to the emergence of a culture-dwelling animal—an animal not bound within a predetermined ecological niche like the tern or the stag or the dragonfly or even the chimpanzee, but, in its very tissues and organs and aptitudes, born to be *open to its world,* to be able to accept responsibility to make its own the traditions of a historical past and to make them into an unforeseeable future. (*AB,* p. 48)

We may reconsider our approach to culture and perception, therefore, from these scientific observations that in our very flesh and bones, our emergence in the womb, and our psychic parturition in the mother's care and love, the creative power of human culture is an integral manifestation of our evolution, and our movement forward to more adequate relationships with the world: our *knowing*. To say this links both science and the arts as ways of trying to make sense of our lives, a way of finding *meaning* in life, which is continually engaged with the world (in this we have something like F. R. Leavis's "living principle"):

> We are always, as human beings, being in a world, in advance of our data in the aspiration to knowledge, yet caught in the ambiguity of our finitude between the explicit surface of our knowledge, the formulable, impersonal aspect of it, and the tacit, often even unknown clues to it in reliance on which we attend to that explicit core. There is no absolute, once for all, knowing by human beings, neither in supernatural confrontation with Really Reals nor in a logical checking off of falsified notknowns. There are only ourselves, using all the means at our disposal: bodily orientation, sensory images, verbal formulations with their over- and under-tones, social taboos and imperatives—including all the lore and practice and procedure of any given discipline we have been trained to—and, finally, our deepest, widest vision of the world we dwell in: using all these as clues to the nature we are in a given instance trying to understand. (*KK*, p. 33)

Knowing is thus bound up with the whole existence of the human being. Moreover, knowledge is inevitable bound up with questions of value and meaning. Some further arguments of Helmuth Plessner as discussed by Marjorie Grene are relevant here. This philosopher of biology puts forward some valuable existential concepts, and he sees the essential creativity of man in his engagement with his reality—an engagement that can never quite bring the fulfillment he seeks, but, through aspiration to the good, *makes* and *reveals* his world.

First of all Helmuth Plessner sees man as a being "who makes demands on himself." With the psychoanalysts, this philosophical biologist sees a man as primarily a *moral* being:

> He is moral (*sittsam*) by nature, an organism which tames itself by making demands on itself, which domesticates itself . . . the essential fact of his positionality becomes what is called conscience, the source from which ethical life and concrete moral existence flow. (Quoted in *AB*, p. 111)[4]

In conscience man expresses both his otherness from nature and his second nature. "He is both alienated from nature, from his own nature, and turned to a higher nature, a contrived nature, in which he becomes himself, in which he is at home." In culture, thus, he transcends "the more pervasive teleology of animal needs." This means that, under the exigencies of the new *biology*, the new *life science*, we are obliged to have the

moral responsibility to resist the pseudo-biological nihilism that predomi-
nates in our culture. With Maslow in *Towards a Psychology of Being*, we
must insist that man has a higher nature that is just as "instinctoid."

Yet man never quite achieves the goods he seeks. Our knowing always
belongs to the tension between appearance and reality, and this paradox is
nonetheless found in our artistic and other cultural efforts. There is always
a discrepancy betwen what we aim at and what we achieve, and all cultural
efforts involve some kind of "compromise with reality." In this Plessner
finds what he calls our "contingency," and our eccentricity.

Another aspect of this eccentricity is what Plessner calls "the utopian
position," in conflict with the actuality of being mortal and insignificant:

> Man stands outside himself; he can do so totally, in the realization of his
> own nothingness or of the nothingness of the world. In his social
> relations, for example, the very fact of community displays his
> nothingness; for he, the individual, is replaceable by his fellow. . . . *One*
> stands for *all*. But that is to deny that one is oneself; and yet one is
> oneself. This paradox . . . underlies our social institutions: we are not
> born into clear, viable relations with others; we have to make them.
> (*AB*, p. 113)

The political and social implications of these new views are wide, and
again, they relate to intentionality. What we should be looking for, trying to
create, is a society in which meaning is at a premium—and in which
meaning can be created, to set against nothingness and death. The focal
point of this creative effort to establish a meaningful world should surely
be in the humanities in education?

The new biologists like Plessner tell us that if we really find our human
biological nature, we shall also find hope and intentionality. The future
tense is restored: "in order to understand how something happens,"
Plessner says, "we must first understand what it is that is to happen." As
Marjorie Grene puts it, "The morphology of human behaviour, both active
and expressive, both goal-directed and intrinsically significant, precedes,
logically and philosophically, the analysis of its physical and biological
conditions" (*AB,* p. 117).

The main tradition of modern Western thought has put the cart before
the horse. We need now to pay attention to such emphases as those of
Plessner which display our continuity with organic nature, and yet our
intrinsic creative difference from it. We need to recognize that "we cannot
analyse successfully the means through which our nature is expressed
until we first understand what that nature is" (ibid.). That sentence alone,
if accepted, should alter our whole approach to the humanities, as in, say,
the education of teachers (and the psychology they are taught). The
explicitness and air of complete certainty sometimes to be found in "ob-

jective" science (though perhaps less nowadays) is spurious: "No such understanding, on the other hand is ever final and complete: it belongs to the very ambiguity of personhood that this is so" (ibid.).

This means that we must live in the half-light of uncertainty in which those working in the arts and humanities have always lived: not least in psychology, sociology, and other such disciplines.[5] To accept this is not to be "irrational," but rather to seek a fuller rationality at last:

> Overcoming both the absurdities of reductivities and the emptiness of idealism, it [Plessner's theory of organic modals] can provide, at long last, a firm rational basis both for the biological sciences, in the many-leveled structure, and for the sciences of man. (*AB*, p. 117)

And, we would hope, for the arts and education of man, too. These remarks by Marjorie Grene show how this kind of phenomenological study is of interest both to science and to art. It also shows how difficult such studies are, yet how creative they can be. The solution to our problems lies in exploring our real nature, in painful awareness (such as we find in much art) that this is a dark, groping, taxing progress. Our reward, however, is the recognition that the mind's element is not eternity, but "the future through which, and towards which it aspires" (*AB*, p. 114).

Because of this, philosophy and psychology must recognize that in the insights of the new form of philosophical biology and phenomenology there are new responsibilities. For the *animal symbolicum*, "the essential fact of his positionality becomes what is called conscience, the source from which ethical life and concrete moral existence flow" (Plessner, quoted in *AB*). We are moral by nature, and this morality is bound up with our capacity to envisage the future and make choices toward it. As Aaron Esterson has put it, "to be human is to be moral."

This is what the new philosophical anthropology, comprising psychoanalysis, Daseinsanalysis,[6] the new existentialism, phenomenology, philosophical biology, and postcritical philosophy, asserts: that man is "both alienated from nature, from his own nature, and turned to higher nature, a contrived nature, in which he becomes himself, in which he is at home." Nor is this just a "compensation for his natural neediness . . . we seek the completion of ourselves . . . not simply through the assuagement of desire but through aspiration to the good" (*AB*, p. 111). As Maslow says, we now need an emphasis, *in the name of realism*, on man's higher nature: and this can be a humanistic, nonreligious emphasis, albeit profoundly concerned with the meaning of life. We are asked to accept it, not because we are exhorted to "have faith" but because it is *true*.

It might seem at first a bad time to attempt such a change of emphasis, but I don't think so. As F. R. Leavis says in *The Living Principle*, "it has become more necessary than it was (in Lawrence's time) to guard the idea of spontaneity against reductive assumptions." The reduction of man to his functions, implicit for example in much psychology and philosophy taught to students and even to student teachers, menaces the future—at a time when the whole tendency of the system of our society (whether in affluence or crisis) is to drive the meaning out of life by implicity reducing man to his functions both in his everyday life and in our philosophical views. A new psychology of being and a philosophical anthropology that can find our creativity are both urgently needed in education. D. H. Lawrence, judging by his depiction of Ursula Brangwen's predicament, would have understood the relevance of the new movement, and because of this I believe the teacher in the humanities will, too.

Notes

1. See his introduction to *Mill on Bentham and Coleridge* and *The Living Principle,* also passim in his literary criticism.

2. See, for example, how "Cambridge positivism" was felt by Kathleen Raine to oppress her, in her autobiographical volumes.

3. See the poems "The Best of School," "Last Lesson of the Afternoon," "A Snowy Day in School," and "Discipline," in *Rhyming Poems.*

4. The original source is *Die Stufen des Organischen und der Mensch* (Berlin: de Gruyter, 1928, 1965).

5. Plessner's *Laughing and Crying* lies between science and the humanities. "The character of both as *reactions to a crisis of human behaviour as such* . . . is the source of the contrast. To be a person . . . is to *be* a body, to *have* a body, *and* to take a stand over against both these and the relation between them."

6. Daseinsanalysis is a form of psychotherapy influenced by the philosophy of Martin Heidegger and his concept of being-unto-death. The human need, it assumes, is for a sensing of "being there," of having achieved some sense of meaning in existence before being swept into nothingness. See *Existence—A New Dimension in Psychiatry and Psychology,* ed. Rollo May et al. (New York: Basic Books, 1958).

3

The Cartesian Limitation

One central issue in our approach to problems of psychology and philosophy is what we believe to be valid truth. In Western traditions of thought there is an astonishing duality—on the one hand intellectual lucidity, and on the other hand dark areas of inner conflict and alienation. This problem may perhaps be traced to the psychological condition of certain key figures in the history of Western thought, notably Descartes, the great mathematician and philosopher whose work made the scientific revolution possible. It is possible that our accustomed view of the world, influenced by him, is a deeply disturbed one.

Descartes split the universe in two—a *res cogitans* (a thinking something with no spatial dimension) and a *res extensa* (a spatial something that has no psychic qualities). If this is a premise for a certain kind of scientific investigation, it is unobjectionable: it was, indeed, the only way the exact sciences could be developed. As Karl Stern puts it in *The Flight from Woman,* the subject had first to leave the stage, so that the world might be elucidated mathematically. While man found himself imbedded in nature and at one with it, as in scholastic times, he could not be scientifically objective. Cartesian dualism was thus a prerequisite for a scientific methodology.

Descartes may be called the founder of modern philosophy. He was a scientist and mathematician, but he was also a believer—indeed, a Catholic. Yet, in his *Rules for the Direction of the Mind,* he argues that there *is* only mathematics:

> arithmetic and geometry alone are free from any taint of falsehood and uncertainty. (Haldane, 1:4)

These "wholly consist in the rational deduction of consequences." Descartes thus set his mark upon the modern intellectual temper; as Marjorie Grene says: "he represents the attitude to knowledge of modern science at its start" (*KK,* p. 64). He was concerned with problem-solving, but at the same time with certainty, "the indubitable and permanent results which

. . . could be obtained by that process [i.e., problem solving] if rightly conceived and rightly pursued." Certainty becomes the primary object of philosophical investigation.

His philosophy put *discovery* at the center of the intellectual stage, and his aim was a "firm and lasting structure in the sciences." His certainty relies neither on a really real beyond the world, nor on *"rootedness in the structure of the world itself."*

> It is the pure, intrinsic certainty of the knowing intellect itself, needing no support beyond the luminous self-evidence of its own act of understanding. (Grene, *KK,* p. 17)

But what happens when the object of scientific attention, as in the life sciences, is a subject, as are all living things? And what happens when Cartesian scientific methodology is extended into a general philosophy of life? It is here that Cartesian attitudes to existence have become disastrous. As Stern says, it implies a fearful estrangement: "Just think of nature as nothing but a huge vastly extended soulless machine which you can take apart experimentally and analyze mathematically, which you can run—but with which you have lost all oneness." (*The Flight from Woman,* p. 76).

Psychologically, such a view of the universe may have its origins in a dark area of personal conflict, as Karl Stern suggests. Descartes contributed to the devaluation of poetic knowledge, and his theory was a step on the road to modern positivism—with its view that a poetic statement has no cognitive validity—toward its culmination in symbolic logic, and its dissociation from life and morality.

Karl Stern points out that the words for *mater* and *materia, mother* and *matter* are all linked etymologically in more than one language. The increasing failure of man to feel at one with Mother Earth and the universe is related to his failure to relate to "the other," and to the feminine.

The view that the whole of nature can be understood only in terms of mathematical relationships belongs to a kind of emotional alienation that has all the features of the schizoid condition of "that utter loss of reality with which a future schizophrenic child looks at his mother. A machine cannot give birth" (Stern, p. 78). The Cartesian ethos, Stern suggests, has a psychological root. Descartes lost his mother when he was little more than a year old. She died in childbirth and the newborn child died with her. I must leave the reader to study the historical account in Stern's book, of Descartes' childhood, his intellectual and cold relationships with women, and his grotesque final fate at the hands of Queen Christina of Sweden. Here are all the manifestations of the schizoid life, leading to a pathological skepticism. "Doubt," says Ernst Cassirer, "is a threat and enemy to the soul . . . for Descartes . . . the radicalism of doubt becomes the only and true source of all knowledge." Thus the origins of modern scientific positivism are in Descartes' schizoid incapacity to trust the world and to find reality. Stern demonstrates how this doubt develops into modern nihilism, if the world is seen only as an "infinitely ambiguous and deceptive creation" the individual comes not only to lose his faith in reason, but "falls into a bottomless abyss, because there is no other bottom but reason to hold him." Descartes thus leads to Nietzsche. Descartes, of course, preserved God; but He became thus already expendable. "He is relegated to the drawing room, a good piece of furniture which the philosopher dusts from time to time" (Stern, p. 102).

Stern argues that, phenomenologically speaking, poetic knowledge is acquired by *union* with and *attachment to* the object: scientific knowledge is acquired by distance and detachment *from* the object. The poetic relation to nature is one of imbeddedness; the scientific one is that of confrontation. Descartes' conception of his method seemed like an incantation. His ideal was the mathematization of all knowledge with an eventual complete *Entseelung,* deanimation of the knowable. It is this impulse to make the world lifeless, eminently schizoid, that broods over the world of modern science. It is also, Stern suggests, a *masculinization* of thought. Descartes belongs to all those developments in our civilization by which we have exploited the male potentialities at the expense of those female element capacities that have to do with at-one-ness and being. Reality becomes a formula, man becomes fleshless, and there is only infinite space to penetrate. By an analysis of Descartes' dreams Karl Stern enables us to see how Descartes' psychopathology lies at the heart of the psychopathology of modern science, with its view of the world and evolution, which retains these disturbed elements.

Existentialism concerns itself with the fact that *Descartes' emphasis came to be upon the disembodied intellect.* To him, knowledge and learning were not *personal.* They were not, as the new existentialism sees them, "achievements of the whole psycho-physical person, making sense of one aspect or another of his situation, of his world" (Grene, *KK,* p. 82). Knowing for him was not a manifestation of *"personhood,* which can entail immense complexities of organisation, many levels of being and achievement . . . never cut off from its contingent, local, bodily root" (ibid. p. 82).

So, through Descartes' influence, knowledge came to be cut off from personal "philosophical space," from belief, from the preoccupation with meaning. Descartes' *cogito ergo sum* is one of the great falsehoods of philosophy, because it implies a clear and immediate knowledge of oneself, when in truth we know ourselves largely by intersubjectivity, by the reflected impact of ourselves on others. We now know how little people know of themselves, and what they *cannot* know, as from psychoanalysis. Much of our primary experience, our indubitable reality, inner and outer, is incapable of being distinctly known.[1]

Descartes falsified heuristics by leading men to feel that they could have "clear and distinct ideas." The whole edifice of scientific belief came to be based on this fundamental notion, as if scientific truths suddenly presented themselves, like something born out of the ear of a goddess, to the mind. Today, where are these clear and distinct ideas in science? There seems to be no "true and evident cognition" even over the fundamental nature of matter: objects are particles on Monday, Wednesday, and Friday and waves on Tuesday and Thursday, and all is misty with quarks and charm. Certainty is not possible, neither with the psychic nor in physics; it is an unreal ideal, only tenable in an intellectual form, and not in the *Lebenswelt*.

In his *Meditation Three* Descartes turns to proving the existence of God by his kind of logic. God must be left intact in the new mathematical universe and so various dodges are necessary to preserve him.

He is trying to prove that God does not deceive him in order that he may henceforth be able to trust his clear and distinct ideas, as before this he could not confidently do. But he uses in his proof principles, like the causal axiom, which he says, he knows "by natural light"—that is, as clear and distinct ideas. Again, he has avowedly discarded all his former opinions in order to build up anew a foundation for the sciences; yet the principles used in this proof look, to us at least, very traditional indeed, just the sort of maxim Descartes would have been taught to accept without the initial critical doubt he so values—and he has by no means discarded them. (Grene, *KK*, p. 72)

Descartes was a good Catholic, and really relied on "revelation" or "intuition" to find God, by a certain kind of attention rather than logical proof.

Turn your mind first from sense to your own conscious being, then from your own conscious being to the idea of an Infinite Being which, Descartes is sure, you innately possess.

As a consequence of these fallacies Descartes came to divide philosophy from religion, and to compartmentalize both. The effect on the morality of our era was seriously damaging. Questions of the meaning of human existence were left to the Church, while philosophy was to concern itself with pure intellectual questions such as the truth and logic of statements, the relationship between the mind and the physical world, and between the mind and the senses. All the puzzlements of the embodied self seeking meaning were excluded from scientific philosophy (even though it might still call itself "moral science"). In universities "natural philosophy" still means Cartesian mathematics and no one may raise the old (poetic) philosophical questions at all. God, however, was neatly stored in a compartment beyond the access of scientific skepticism (where ultimately He has died).

Existentialism challenges this compartmentalized view of knowing on the one hand, and the idea of "clear and distinct" knowing on the other. One of the serious consequences of the Cartesian view has been a failure to see that learning has a forward-moving quality, that "knowledge is an achievement, but like every living achievement a stage in history, neither an end nor simply a beginning, but a 'stage on life's way.'" There can be no wholly focal knowledge:

> The idea of wholly explicit, wholly certifying truth, ignoring this insight, falsifies at once the nature of the knower and the known, of mind and the world. (Grene, *KK*, p. 91)

Descartes' falsifications, however, still color the work of science, when it is faced with the "category of life," especially in much psychology. The point may be emphasized by some quotations from the phenomenologist Merleau-Ponty and a reference to the problem of time. Descartes' world of 'certainties' is atemporal: it consists of spatial relations on the one hand and the geometer's understanding of them on the other. Time for Descartes was a series of independent instants and it needed God's effort to keep the world in being from one moment to the next. Each instant in Descartes' time is independent: but if we think about it, moving with a ruler or micrometer from one point to another involves us in dimensions of space and time that make this approach inadequate, for times does not consist of little beads strung together like that. Descartes' self and world are almost like the infant's before he comes together as one self in one world, recognizably schizoid, like the world of *Alice in Wonderland*. We know we are always moving about the world in the continuous flux of time, in a continuous body, and in this time and space we exercise our consciousness in "intentionalities." Merleau-Ponty quotes Husserl:

> Husserl uses the terms protentions and retentions for the intentionalities which anchor one to an environment. They do not run from a central I, but from my perceptual field itself, so to speak, which draws along in its wake its own horizon of retentions, and bites into the future with its protentions. I do not pass through a series of instances of now, the images of which I preserve and which placed end to end, make a line. (*Phenomenology of Perception*, p. 416)

The intellectualized Cartesian model of the self-in-time thus oversimplifies a very complex and dynamic relation between ourselves and the flux. But Descartes deprived man, by his emphasis on mathematical certainty, his fragmented time, and his concept of clear and immediate knowing, of a much richer and more dynamic sense of the activity of exploring and knowing. He managed to cut man off from his deeper embodied perplexities as a whole knower, and from those questions which belong to our moral being, and our quest for meaning, as in religion. The effect has been to leave us in serious difficulties about time and creativity in time. This is the "crime" of which Lewis Mumford accuses Descartes.

In the anti-Cartesian movement, there is a new emphasis on *process.*

> We are always beyond ourselves in the venture of knowing, the task of finding and giving as best we can significance to our world, the world which is always beyond us at the horizon, but whose concrescence, whose interpretation, whose meaning we are. (Grene, *KK*, p. 91)

To quote Merleau-Ponty again: once we escape from the "Cartesian string of bead-like instants" we find

> time is the foundation and measure of our spontaneity, and the power of out-running and of "néantiser"* which dwells within us and is our-selves, is itself given to us with temporality and life. (*Phenomenology of Perception,* p. 428)

---

*producing a negative entity.

"We are not in some incomprehensible way an activity joined to a passivity, an automatism surmounted by a will, a perception surmounted by a judgment, but wholly active and wholly passive, because we *are the upsurge of time*" (ibid., p. 41, emphasis added). While we may not quite understand those marvelous passages from the French phenomenologist, we can perhaps grasp that they are directed at overcoming those approaches to human problems which (as in behaviorism) lack all recognition of creative dynamics, or even of problems of subjectivity and intersubjectivity: "We are not pure cognitions absurdly attached to a machine."

Knowledge cannot be separated from those problems which Descartes thrust aside as the province of religion, mind cannot be understood apart from body, nor from the whole being-in-the-world in time, rooted in his condition and historical moment. If these separations are made, we become threatened with menaces to our essential freedom, as in behaviourism.

The philosophical tradition inspired by Descartes has tried to "seek a pure and independent Reason exempt from the hazards of life":

what Cartesianism prevents, in the last analysis, is the mediation be-tween mind and nature through the concept of *life*. (Grene, *KK*, p. 147)

Grene links this with the impulses of reductionism. She quotes Henry Oldenberg writing to Spinoza about the Royal Society: "all the effects of Nature are produced by motion, figure, texture, and the varying combina-tion of these." "Specify the parts," she says, "and you have the whole."

> The parts of an organism are chemical molecules; specify these and you need worry about "life" no longer.
> But parts by definition are *of* a whole and as genetical research proceeds . . . the nature of the whole, too, makes itself felt. (Ibid., p. 208)

Here there is an enormous reaction under way, toward a new holism.[2]

In the new philosophical anthropology there is a movement to make good the damage Descartes caused, by restoring the sense of entities:

> To know life is to comprehend comprehensive entities: to know knowing is to comprehend those particular achievements of living things which consist in their acts of comprehension. (Grene, *KK*, p. 224)

And since, with man, this comprehension involves "intentionality" and thus creativity, the anti-Cartesian movement is a process of recovering human freedom, which was seriously damaged by the Cartesian legacy.

Here the work of Marjorie Grene is of great importance, and I believe that she has been able to make a special contribution because she is a woman. A woman seems less willing to forfeit female modes of knowing under the domination of the masculinization of knowledge. In her chapter "The Errors of Descartes" (in KK), and her chapter on Adolf Portmann in *Approaches to a Philosophical Biology* she deals with the hostility of Galileo to the poetic, and both chapters seem to spring from feminine insights into this tendency. Her aim in the latter work is to help to emancipate those disciplines which deal with living subjects "from the bones of a rigid, physics-dominated metaphysics that has too long held them captive,"—that is, from the masculinization of knowledge itself.

Perhaps the most fundamental issue in this philosophical debate is the rejection by the Galilean scientific revolution of "secondary qualities" such as color, smell, stickiness, taste, in favor of "primary" qualities such as motion, shape, and the solid resistance of bodies. In modern science "nature is written in the mathematical language," in Galileo's terms:

> Philosophy is written in this great book, the universe, which stand continually open to our gaze. But the book cannot be understood unless

one first learns to comprehend the letters in which it is composed. It is written in the language of mathematics, and its characters are triangles, circles and other geometric figures without which it is humanly impossible to understand a single word of it: without these, one wanders about in a dark labyrinth. (Drake, ed., *Discoveries and Opinions of Galileo*, pp. 237–38)

This is now a truism, and applied mathematics is *the* paradigm of science, while physical science of this kind is *the* paradigm of knowledge. In some we find the firm conviction that, someday, all we know or can know will be statable in strict mathematical form.

But this Galilean learning is not that of the "life-world" in which we know the world, but belongs to a secondary, painfully constructed world of learning, and it requires an abstract secret code, that of mathematics.

Is it true that we can know nature only like that? Compare, for instance, the way in which George Crabbe knew nature, or Farbre studied his insects?[3] Are our apprehensions of color, smell, and sound less substantial than our apprehension of the abstract entities of empiricism?

First, it must be insisted that this strict scientific knowledge grew out of the life-world: the *Weltwissen* (in Husserl's terms) grew out of the *Welterleben*. We each of us have a biological environment, our own space, and within this primary frame but transcending it, we acquire the intellectual systems of modern "objective" thought. But we also in a sense come to *dwell in* the cultural heritage, assimilating it into our whole feeling about the world. We identify it with our primary world, and with reality itself. So in the ethos of Cambridge positivism the Newtonian, Cartesian, Galilean world of the sciences, even despite their fifty-fifty relationship with the Arts, sees to *be* that world which is the object of the attention of the radio-telescopes, electron-microscopes, and pipettes in the laboratories:

So nature comes to *mean* to us Galilean nature and the existence of the primary life-world is ignored. (Grene, *AB*, p. 13)

This primary life-world comprises our feelings about our bodies, our hopes and desires, our irritation with our children, our hunger, our weariness after cutting the grass, the smell of newly dug potatoes, our sexual experience, our alarm at thunder or a gale, the excitement of seeing a bevy of partridges in the garden, our delight in flowers, our experience of *Nicholas Nickleby* or a Mozart horn concerto. All these shape our ongoing experience and are real to us, as the astronomy- or physics-based truths are not.

The "facts" of science—for instance, the structure of large molecules, or the nature of black holes—are *not* our life-world. They are aspects of the reality of the universe conceived of often in terms of very special techniques of measurement, or indeed sometimes by pure speculative thought. But because of the authority that science has in our civilization, these intellectual abstractions tend to dominate our thinking, and come to be extended into a general philosophy.

So we tend to think of our destiny, and even of our morality, on the basis of highly specialized scientific facts, rather than on our direct experience of nature and life. For some this provokes a profound crisis.[4]

A further point made by Marjorie Grene is that modern man, by isolating himself from the natural world, and by technology, has come to deny the existence of nature in the primary sense, in an ultra-Galilean way. While the abstract language of mathematics may be the only language of nature he has learned, there is another natural pattern to which he belongs. Again, we have the problem of the concept of ourselves within which we work. But today's city-dweller, not least through his education, the objective world of science and technology comes to be identified with "nature": if he seeks to study nature he will buy a "nature book" or watch a "nature film." "Nature loving" is fast becoming yet another commodity; yet we suffer from a radical inability to find our place in nature, a way of being-in-the-world, of belonging to Nature. This is a philosophical problem, but has also become a problem of our way of life, as conservation issues make clear.

The equating of "nature" with the objects of science, and the alienation of modern man from nature, make it difficult for us to make the proper kind of necessary conceptual reexamination of Galileo's legacy. We have to strive to reintegrate man into nature, and in this we have to strive against a whole era of the rejection of the poetic, which meant really a rejection of the subjective life and our natural culture, which (as the poets instruct us) are valid ways of achieving a sense of at-one-ness with nature.

In *The Assayer* Galileo clearly rejects the poetic. As Marjorie Grene shows, he also rejects the existence of colors, sounds, odors, and the like in nature. He tries to declare that there is *only* mathematics in nature and nothing else, and where we have gone astray is in following him into this, without thinking enough about the distinctions he makes:

> Now I say that whenever I conceive any material or corporeal substance, I immediately feel the need to think of it as bounded, and as having this or that shape; as being large and small in relation to other things, and in some specific place at any given time; as being in motion or at rest; as touching or not touching some other body; and as being one in number, or few, or many. From these conditions I cannot separate such a substance by any stretch of my imagination.[5]

This seems clear enough: one cannot conceive of objects without supposing that they occupy space and stand in relation to one another. This is the basis of physics. But Galileo goes on to claim that the mathematically measurable properties are the *only* real ones:

> But that it must be white or red, bitter or sweet, noisy or silent, or of sweel or foul odor, my mind does not feel compelled to bring in as necessary accompaniments. Without the senses as our guides, reason or imagination unaided would probably never arrive at qualities like these. (Ibid.)

The senses, belonging to the (sinful) body, and to deception, the area of poetry, do not really apprehend a real world. Reason and imagination are for him a form of direct clear knowledge going straight to the primary properties, which can be mathematically expressed. Those secondary properties (which one can feel and experience even as one writes a philosophical argument, striking the eye from one's telephone and pullover, echoing in one's ear from the cat and the cars outside, pressing against one's bottom from the chair seat) *do not exist at all,* and what *does* exist in the only way to be trusted is the distance between one's cup and inkwell, and the weight of the pen in one's hand:

> Hence I think that tastes, odors, colors, and so on are no more than mere names so far as the object in which we place them is concerned, and that they reside only in the consciousness. (Ibid.)

The question arises, of course, *where do the primary properties reside if not in the consciousness?* Galileo goes on:

> Hence, If the living creatures were removed, all these qualities would be wiped away and annihilated.

But what would happen to the primary qualities, too, if all the living creatures were removed? The sun might go on being big and more or less round, but it would not be *known* and could not be described. Knowledge exists only in consciousness, too: it is this emphasis that makes the work of Michael Polanyi so important. Oddly enough, in his skepticism, Descartes did discover consciousness—it was, in a sense, all that he could rely on. He declared himself determined

> never to accept anything for true which I did not clearly know to be such: that is to say, carefully to avoid precipitancy and prejudice, and to comprise nothing more in my judgement than what was presented to my mind so clearly and distinctly as to enclose all ground of doubt. (*Discours de la Méthode,* pt. 2)

He is to doubt, deliberately, the existence of everything until he arrived at something indubitable. But what he cannot doubt is his own existence:

And what, essentially, is this "I"? A *thinking* thing; *cogito, ergo sum*.

Descartes concludes not only that this consciousness of self-existence is the first and most indubitable of all truths:

but I, as a *thinking* being, must be of a non-material nature.

From this arises the deepest errors of Descartes. For Descartes finds the clear and distinct apprehensions of the mind "true" only because the senses can be deceived:

He decided that *whatever is clearly and distinctly apprehended is true.*

The ideas our senses offer us are not clear and distinct, so not true. Can he discover any idea that is clear and distinct? Descartes decides that God is such an idea,

the idea of a being more perfect that myself must of necessity have proceeded from a being in reality more perfect.

As Basil Willey pointed out, Keats's view of the relationship between the "I" and the world is totally different from that of Descartes, with his distrust and his flight into abstraction. For Keats declared,

I can never understand how anything can be *known for truth* by a process of abstract reasoning.

Descartes, having established intellectually that God exists, could, as it were, "allow" the existence of material things; but the only properties of these that he can recognize as *true* are the *mathematical properties:*

It is at least necessary to admit that all which I clearly and distinctly conceive as in them, that is, generally speaking, all that is comprehended in the object of speculative geometry, really exists external to me. *(Sixth Meditation)*

The trouble is that, as Husserl says, "The arithmetical world is there for me only when and so long as I occupy the world in the ordinary sense of the word, is *constantly* there for me, so long as I live naturally and look in its direction. . . . It is then to this world, the *world in which I find myself and which is also my world about me,* that my manifold and shifting spontaneities of consciousness stand related." But to Descartes only the objects of mathematical thought were real: *(Ideas, p. 93)*

My certainty of my own existence, then, and my certainty of God's existence, are the two first certainties: from these we can also derive certainty that the objects of mathematical thought are real. (Willey, *Seventeenth-Century Background*, p. 85)

However, as Marjorie Grene points out, herein lies Descartes' other profound error—for mathematical thought can yield *no certainties whatever*. The consequences in science are still with us. As Susanne Langer says:

No schoolman speculating on essences and attributes ever approached anything like the abstractions of algebra. Yet those same scientists who prided themselves on their concrete factual knowledge, who claimed to reject every proof except empirical evidence, never hesitated to accept the demonstrations and calculations, the bodiless, sometimes avowedly "fictitious" entites of the mathematicians. . . . why are their abstractions taken not only seriously, but as indispensable, fundamental facts . . .? (*Philosophy in a New Key*, p. 18)

What the new disciplines of philosophical anthropology are trying to indicate is that the established distrust of "the poetic" in our Western modes of thought is unjustified. As the work of Susanne Langer herself shows, symbolism is the basis of all thought, and that this is so reveals that, in both scientific thinking and in the poetic disciplines, human beings are trying to understand the world through metaphor. To attribute reality to only one of the two worlds of ὕπαρ and ὄναρ, and to dismiss the one as "pure illusion" was a serious mistake. Dreams, as E. R. Dodds puts it, "are highly significant after all," as psychoanalysis has shown, and our need for seeking meaning through vision and dream is shown by existentialist psychotherapy to be a primary need, as valuable as science in making sense of our world.

Descartes divided reality into two substances—thought and extensions. On the one hand, soul or mind, distinct from the body and not in touch with matter, the true "thinking substances": and on the other hand, matter-in-motion out there, mathematical objects obeying mechanical laws. But what was the bridge between these? As Willey says, "strange devices had to be resorted to in order to link together what God had joined and philosophers had put asunder." Descartes' only answer was the pineal gland!

The secret of Cartesian method is to order such acts of understanding by "the undoubting conception of a pure and attentive mind." In an intellectual act that in contrast to "the fluctuating testimony of the senses," or "the misleading judgement that proceeds from the blundering constructions of imagination," he "frees us wholly from doubt about that which we understand."

Descartes assumed that we could arrive at "a unified, all-embracing body of . . . knowledge," so that we could, within a couple of generations, solve all the problems that will ever confront the human mind. But where is the march straight forward from certainty to certainty? Where is apodicity? In the advance of knowledge, the entanglement of truth and error, and of success and failure, are inextricable.

Of course, some discoveries have to all intents and purposes an air of once-for-all established truth. But the "facts" of science do not have the certainty (as Descartes thought) of "logical necessity": they are "contingent facts of our cosmic epoch" since science is only scientists doing something—one trying to make sense of their experience. So those concerned with the structure of knowledge must still insist on the want of logical certainty, the absence of "Cartesian self-evidence, characteristic of even the least doubtful of established truths."

We can never withdraw . . . one item of "information" and say of it, this, all on its own, is so luminous, so firmly established, that it could not conceivably be otherwise. . . . It is a condition of our "Geworfenheit" [Heidegger—being "thrown into the world"], of the world into which we are cast, and we forget at our peril its ultimate contingency. (*KK,* p. 75)

Marjorie Grene's objection is that Descartes "unnecessarily psychologised mathematical certainty, which is that of an inference machine or computer, not that of a thinking mind." Moreover, the scientist in his wake has wrongly extrapolated mathematical certainty to the domain of experimental science, which is properly that of probabilities, not of certainties. So, Descartes' certainties are in the end chimerical:

the study of mathematical heuristics, far from exhibiting a clear path of certainty, demonstrates that hunches, the imaginative use of example, definition and re-definition, sheer irrational preference or prejudice, enter essentially and centrally into the reasonings of mathematicians just as they do in any other process of learning or discovery. The fact that mathematical concepts are simple and more precise—or less imprecise—that more everyday concepts, does not mean, as Descartes thought it did, that in mathematics, one has left the plane of fallibility, of gropings, of half-lights, of puzzles wrongly solved and tried again, for some utopian and infallible truth. *There is no such place.* True the prepositions asserted by mathematicians *claim,* like all universal propositions, universal validity. But the claim, however strong, is always rooted in the confidence of those who make it. Mathematicians, like other people, are trying to make sense of an aspect of experience: trying to find a pattern in what is otherwise disorder . . . they are still groping, seeking, and finding understanding: not *the* truth, but a claim to truth, still anchored in their personal intellectual situation, in their orientation in the world. (*KK,* p. 77, emphasis added)

This, again, is an existentialist emphasis. There are no "clear and distinct ideas"; even in mathematics there are only human beings trying to make sense of their experience. And this attempt to make sense of the world is a manifestation of freedom and responsibility. Here we return to the theme of intentionality, and must consider the effects of Descartes on freedom. Rollo May says:

> Intentionality, in human experience, is what underlies will and decision. It is not only prior to will and decision but makes them possible. Why it has been neglected in Western history is clear enough. Ever since Descartes separated understanding from will, science has progressed on the basis of this dichotomy, and we tried to assume that "facts" about human beings could be separated from their "freedom," cognition could be separated from conation. Particularly since Freud, this is no longer possible—even though Freud, without full justice to his own discoveries, clung to the old dichotomy in scientific theory. Intentionality does not rule out deterministic influence, but placed the whole problem of determinism and freedom on a deeper plane. (*LW*, p. 210)[6]

If we do not see these dimensions, we lose all effectiveness. Descartes "was contributing an essential ingredient to the growth of the idea of progress." But at a cost, as Karl Stern makes clear: the alienation he promoted, making us seem victims of the universe machine, was a serious menace to our sense of the validity and meaningfulness of our lives.

In psychology there needs to be especially a radical reconsideration of how we know and what we know. In Marjorie Grene's terms, we must "work back to the source of encounter as a way of being-in-the-world," and this involves us in examining the whole problem of reciprocity and its origins. Certainly, in knowing about man, we must be ready for "meeting": "already there, inviting encounter, the other person comes into view, as a question expecting an answer." That is, the other person doesn't exist in our investigation until we creatively reflect him, and enter into encounter with him. In this, his inward life and ours are significant, as are our expectations of what answer will be given one to the other. Each lives in a life-world. "Every person chooses his way of being in the world: he makes his world the world it is by his projection of it." The "externally given," what is objectively present, is a necessary point of reference within the structure of being-in-the-world. And as Marjorie Grene suggests, "encounter demands a certain reciprocity."

Once we accept the concept of reciprocity, it becomes evident that any form of meeting between human beings has in it elements of "indwelling" that can affect perception in the deepest way because we are not simply "spatio-temporarily perceived objects, but persons."

In this search for a new way of knowing man, we are inevitably anti-Cartesian. We are so used to the Cartesian falsification that we do not notice it; even as in the work of psychologists, sociologists, and the planning and teaching based on their work, man suffers from the Cartesian limitations.

Science continues to base its concepts of knowledge on Descartes' concepts of "clear and distinct ideas." Our society believes that it can still solve the world's problems in that dimension, by that apodicity. If we examine many university prospectuses we shall see that nearly everything in them belongs to the world of "objectivity" and assumes that measuring and manipulation in the positivist paradigm are the ways to deal with the world.

Even in the humanities there presses upon us the feeling that we must establish our "authenticity" on verifiable "empirical" and "objective" studies. Even in the study of man and society, the prevailing mode is that of science trying to be as objective as possible, in which process the more the "subjective" elements are excluded, the better, it would seem. Yet a book like Peter Abbs's *Autobiography in Education,* which seeks to draw from students their subjective experience, in order to try to organize it and understand their experience, offers so much more than many books on education. Even in English there are trends toward approaches that seem to display a Cartesian authenticity, as in the attempts to apply linguistics theory or abstract literary theory to the study of literature. In sociobiology we even have it suggested that a biology of particulate analysis is a sounder basis for the humanities and even ethics, as in the works of E. O. Wilson. The inner life of man, his cultural dimension, his creative power, his intentionality, his preoccupation with the meaning of his life and with values, may be missing altogether from the syllabus as fit areas of study. In the general Cartesian atmosphere, these questions are not felt to be real ones. For parallel reasons the politicians feel that they must demand "realism" or "vocational relevance"—and propose that disciplines concerned with problems of consciousness, culture, and meaning may be deliberately run down. To this process established psychology and philosophy seem to have no grounds for resistance.

Yet, on the Continent and in America, there is a considerable long-established, anti-Cartesian movement, toward a more adequate approach to the problems of philosophy and psychology, hence to a brief historical survey of this movement we now turn.

Notes

1. See, for example, Michael Polanyi, *The Study of Man* (Chicago: University of Chicago Press, 1958), a brief introduction to his *Personal Knowledge.*

2. See Marjorie Grene, *The Understanding of Nature.* The English specialist will understand the relevance of the philosophical emphases here to F. R. Leavis's continual reiteration throughout his work that " 'life' is a necessary word." See also the first two chapters of E. W. F. Tomlin, *Psyche, Culture and the New Science* (London: Routledge and Kegan Paul, 1985).

3. I have just heard a naturalist speak on the radio of how you need, in studying foxes, to "get right inside the skin of the fox." Hardly a strictly positivist, empirical procedure!

4. The most critical area here is that of the new technology of dealing with the embryo. At what stage does "life" begin? Is the embryo a mere "blob of cells"? Or is it a being? The problem of finding life as real is avoided by absurd solutions to the problem, such as declaring a foetus a being at, say, fourteen days. The dimension of the potentialities inherent in the "primary consciousness" of development is not found. See the present author on "Medical Ethics and the Potentialities of the Living Being," *The British Medical Journal* 291 (1985): 459.

5. See S. Drake, ed., *Discoveries and Opinions of Galileo*, p. 272. Quoted by Marjorie Grene, *AB*, p. 14. The above quotation is from *Il Saggiatore*.

6. See also May's chap. 9, "Intentionality."

4

A Hundred Years of Philosophical Anthropology: A Historical Survey

Philosophical anthropology not only began over a hundred years ago, but began within the context of science itself. Phenomenology grew out of a more general attempt in Europe to develop a widened conception of experience than a sensation-bound positivism allowed for. To understand what might be meant by "sensation bound" we can turn to Hume's view of the mind, which is characteristic of the whole approach to man of the scientific revolution: the self is a bundle of impressions, associative mechanisms; bits of sensation in bits of time, not connected by a continuous "I," to be studied by atomistic microanalysis. As Marjorie Grene argues, Hume's system presides over the trivialization of philosophy, which becomes word games rooted in Humean skepticism (*KK,* pp. 108ff). This philosophical inadequacy is clear in Russell's logic, Dewey's pragmatism, and much of the predominant philosophy of our science. The mind as *knower* is not "there."

The motto put forward by Husserl, "Back to the things themselves," involved a turning away from mere abstract concepts and theories toward the "directly presented" in all its fullness. It will be noted by those working in English and the humanities that this "directly presented" account of existence is what the arts might be said to present at best for it is through art and literature that one centers into the realities of the human consciousness in all its fullness. Our scope is the truth of experience.

One of the forerunners of phenomenology was Franz Brentano (1838–1917). He sought a scientific foundation for a new philosophy, including ethics; but he also sought to devise a "descriptive psychology" by contrast with "genetic psychology," which was to deal with causal explanations. In such acts as perceiving, imagining, judging, and willing, Brentano postulated a new dimension, "Intentionality," and this became a major feature of Husserl's thinking. Brentano also influenced Karl Stumpf (1848–1939), who was essentially an experimental psychologist, but one whose experiments were not concerned with correlations between physical stim-

Historical Chart

Fore-runners

Wilhelm DILTHEY (1833-1911)
  Sought an adequate scientific
  foundation for the *Geisteswissenschaften*.
  UNIVERSITY OF BERLIN C1894

Carl STUMPF (1848-1936)
Interested in experimental phenomenolo[gy]
UNIVERSITY OF BERLIN C1900

Theodore LIPPS (1851-1910) •••••••••••••••••Franz BRENTANO (1838-1917)
  Originator of theory of empathy.   Sought a scientific reformation of philosophy.
  UNIVERSITY OF MUNICH   Tried to develop a descriptive psychology.

*Alexander PFÄNDER (1870-1941)   UNIVERSITY OF VIENNA

*Adolf REINACH (1883-1917)

Alexius MEINONG (1853-1930)
Gestandtheorie or theory of object[s]
sympathetically reviewed by Bertr[and]
German Phenomenologists.   *Edmund HUSSERL (1859-1917)   Russel in *Mind*, 1904.
  UNIVERSITY OF HALLE (1881-1901)   UNIVERSITY OF GRAZ

*Martin HEIDEGGER (1889-1976)   *Max SCHELER (1874-1928)
Sein Und Zeit, 1927

*=Editors of Husserl's
Phenomenological Yearb[ook]
1913-1930

European Influences on Existentialism

Søren KIERKEGAARD (1813-1855)   Sigmund FREUD (1866-1939)   Frederick NIETZSCHE (1844-19[00])

•••••••••••Karl JASPERS (1885-1969)   Martin BUBER (1878-1965)

French Phase

Gabriel MARCEL (1889-1973) --------------------Jean-Paul SARTRE (b.1905)
  Journal Métaphysique, 1927
Maurice MERLEAU-PONTY (1908-1961)
Phénoménologie de la Perception, 1945

Paul RICOEUR (b.1913)
Philosophie de la Volonté, 1950

AMERICA
William JAMES
(1842-19[10])

Recent Developments

NETHERLANDS
F. J. J. BUYTENDIJK (b.1887)

UNITED STATES
Marvin FARBER (b.1901)
John WILD (b.1902)
Gordon ALLPORT
Herbert SPIEGELBERG
Aron GURWITSCH
Paul TILLICH
Rollo MAY
Erwin STRAUS
Kurt GOLDSTEIN
Marjorie GRENE

GERMANY
V. VON WEIZSÄCKER
Adolf PORTMANN
Helmuth PLESSNER
(PUPIL OF HUSSERL)

GREAT BRITAIN
Michael POLANYI
R. D. LAING
Aaron ESTERSON
  D. W. WINNICOTT
  Peter LOMAS
  Marion MILNER

GERMANY
Alfred SCHUTZ

SWITZERLAND
Ludwig BINSWANGER (b.18[81])
Roland KUHN (b.1912)
Medard BOSS

SPAIN
José ORTEGA Y GASSET

FRANCE
E. MINKOWSKI

••••••••••*LINES OF INTERES*[T]
--------*LINES OF FRIENDS*[HIP]
————————*STUDENT-TEACHE*[R]
RELATIONS

Based on the chronological chart
in *Phenomenology in Psychology and
Psychiatry*. Herbert Spiegelberg. Northwestern. 1972

uli and psychological responses but the discriminating and controlled exploration of the subjective phenomena, in a way that makes their reproduction and checking possible even on an intersubjective basis.[1]

Edmund Husserl (1859–1938) was a student of Brentano. When he began, he thought of himself as a descriptive psychologist. His beginnings, actually, were strangely paradoxical. At first he sought to emancipate "pure logic" from psychology and he also fought against psychologism—both (as Spiegelberg says) at the farthest remove from actual psychology. But the search for a new foundation for his new logic in a non-psychological phenomenology "led him back to the abandoned site." Before we can place Husserl, however, we have to look at his historical setting, his teachers, and his connections.

Husserl's position between psychology and philosophy is still being defined. Here we have to make two major efforts of comprehension. One is to explore the development in certain areas of Continental philosophy as yet hardly recognized in Britain or the United States. The other is to grasp the implications of Husserl's injunction, and then (of course) bring this to bear on problems of culture, education, and thought. In Husserl's philosophy the basic fact of pure psychology is consciousness, and this offered a challenge to both philosophy and psychology as they were them. Those involved in the necessary reconsiderations were Brentano, Stumpf, Buhler, Dilthey, and Lipps. Their interrelations may be studied in the Historical Flow Chart presented on the opposite page. Cassirer refers to Dilthey in his discussion of history, his first reference occurring in connection with his treatment of *the crisis in man's knowledge of himself* (chap. 1). It is with this crisis that we are concerned, and it is, of course, the subject of Husserl's main book. Both thinkers return to contemplate the impulse of Greek thought. As we have seen, Cassirer says that the Socratic dialogues show that "knowledge of human nature cannot be gained except through a constant co-operation of the subjects in mutual interrogation and reply." It is by the fundamental faculty of giving a response to himself and to others that man becomes a "responsible" subject, a moral subject, as we have seen.

So, as Cassirer says, "the Socratic problem and the Socratic method can never be forgotten or obliterated." Through the Socratic problem and the Socratic method Platonic thought has left its mark on the whole future development of human civilization.

Cassirer says at this point that he is not going to attempt a survey of the historical development of *anthropological philosophy,* though "the history of the philosophy of man is still a desideratum." The history of metaphysics, of natural philosophy, of ethical and scientific thought has all been studied in detail. But in the area of philosophical anthropology *"we are here still at the beginning."*

The importance of this problem was felt more strongly in the last century in Europe, and this brings us to Wilhem Dilthey (1833–1911), who concentrated all his efforts on its solution. I first came across the name of Dilthey coupled as on the chart with that of Theodore Lipps (1851–1910) in Michael Polanyi's book, *The Tacit Dimension.*

At the turn of the century, German thinkers postulated that indwelling, or empathy, is the proper means of knowing man and the humanities. I am referring particularly to Dilthey and Lipps.[2]

Dilthey, says Polanyi, taught that the mind of a person can be "understood only be reliving its workings," and Lipps represented aesthetic appreciation as "an entering into a work of art and thus dwelling in the mind of its creator."

I think that Dilthey and Lipps described here a striking form of tacit knowing as applied to the understanding of man and of works of art, and that they were right in saying that this could be achieved only be *indwelling.* (P. 17, emphasis added)

The concept of *indwelling* is important in the new subjective disciplines, as we shall see. As early as 1965 Dilthey was searching for a *reale Psychologie* that could serve as the foundation for the human studies *(Geisteswissenschaften)*—a radically new psychology, which in the *Ideen* of 1894 he terms a "descriptive and analytic psychology," as opposed to the "explanatory psychology" of the physicists. He had high hopes that Husserl's phenomenology could aid him in his attempt to develop this new psychology.

Dilthey failed, and indeed, one may trace the whole history of phenomenology as a series of glorious failures; but even in the original squabbles one can trace the fundamental issues with which we are struggling today. Georg Muller (1850–1935), for example, a leading German experimental psychologist in Göttingen was anti-philosophical and referred to Husserl's philosophy as *Wortklauberei* (verbal hair-splitting); even though his themes come very near to those of Husserl, he never mentions his name. As Cassirer says, "the history of philosophical anthropology is fraught with the deepest human passions and emotions."[3]

In a useful article on *Dilthey and Husserl,* Mary Katherine Tillman gives an account of the interest Husserl displayed in Dilthey's work. In the summer of 1925 Husserl gave his lectures on *Phänomenologische Psychologie.* In this he described W. Dilthey's *Ideen Uber eine beschreibende und zergliedende Psychologie* (1894) as a work of genius in its attack on naturalistic psychology ("a work of genius, although not fully mature, which will certainly remain unforgotten in the history of psychology").

Dilthey's strength, Husserl thought, was in the realm of the concrete life of the spirit, the individual, and the sociohistorical dimension in living con-cretions, its typical forms and purposeful structures. He was known for his concern for *a scientific foundation for the human studies,* and realized that *the new experimental psychology was hopelessly inadequate for such a foundational tasks.* The problem we are tackling thus is a long-standing one, with its origins in these first conflicts between the natural-science empirical scientists, and philosophical anthropologists who suspected the falsities in their work.

In his *Phenomenological Psychology,* Husserl summarizes Dilthey's position and makes clear his distinctions between a causal, constructive, and *explanatory* psychology, and a *descriptive* and analytic psychology, which begins in inner lived experience and the intuition of the whole, the living context.

> In a shorter formulation: natural-scientific understanding. (P. 9)

Not only is there a difference, however, between *Naturwissenschaft* and *Geisteswissenschaft,* the latter requiring *Verstehen* (understanding) by contrast with *Erklarung* (explanation), but there is also the need to de-velop a *Lebensphilosophie*—an understanding of the nature of the general category of *things alive*. As Husserl suggests, Dilthey's insights came too soon for their time; they are only now being painfully explored.

> In our time we everywhere meet the burning need for an understanding of spirit, while the unclarity of the methodological and factual connec-tion between the natural sciences and the sciences of the spirit, has become almost unbearable. Dilthey, one of the greatest scientists of the Spirit, has directed his whole vital energy to clarifying the connection between nature and spirit, to classifying the role of psycho-physical psychology, which he thinks is to be complemented by a new, descrip-tive and analogic psychology.[4]

Two problems were raised by Dilthey about which debate continues: the nature of *history,* and the relationship between *nature and human nature*. To take the first point first. Dilthey emphasizes the autonomy of history, its irreducibility to natural science, its character as *Geisteswissenschaft*. Ernst Cassirer, in his chapter on history in *An Essay on Man,* compares the view of Taine, at least in theory. Taine's view of history was that the historian must collect the "facts" and must investigate their causes. But in practice he admitted that it was impossible to "reduce" historical thought to the method of scientific thought. As Cassirer says:

> If we were to know all the laws of nature, if we could apply to man all our statistical, economic, social rules, still this would not help us to

"see" man in [his] special aspect and in his individual form. Here we are not moving in a physical but a symbolic universe. And for understanding and interpreting symbols we have to develop other methods than those of research into causes. (*EM*, p. 195)

Cassirer here quotes a relevant passage from Taine: "What is your first remark," he asks,

on turning over the great, stiff leaves of a folio, the yellow sheets of a manuscript—a poem, a code of laws, a declaration of faith? This, you say, was not created alone. It is but a mould, like a fossil shell, an imprint, like one of those shapes embossed in stone by an animal which lived and perished. Under the shell there was an animal, and behind the document was a man. Why do you study the shell, except to represent to yourself the animal? So why do you study the document only in order to know the man. . . . we must reach back to this existence, endeavour to re-create it. . . . language, a legislation, a catechism is never more than an abstract thing; the complete thing is the man who acts, the man corporal and visible, who eats, walks, fights, labours. (*EM*, pp. 194–95)

If we seek a general heading under which we are to subsume historical knowledge, we may describe it not as a branch of physics but as a branch of semantics. History is included in the field of hermeneutics, not in that of natural science. The "facts" of history have to be reconstructed by the interpretation of symbols; they cannot be collected from what is observable, as in physics and chemistry. This Taine could not see, despite his implicit admission of the problem in the above passage. Dilthey, on his part, while insisting on the irreducibility of history to a science, left nature as the backdrop against which the human drama was played out, and this backdrop was as it was *explained by the natural sciences*. The historian needs to *understand* actions, aspirations, decision of human beings; the scientist *explains* phenomena.

This attempt by Dilthey to distinguish between the exact sciences and their subject matter on the one hand, and the historical and human disciplines on the other, quite distinct from science with their own characteristic methods, did not solve the problems. Discussing Helmuth Plessner's view of all this, Marjorie Grene points out that a conflict between two spheres like those of nature and history cannot be resolved by setting the two over against one another. We need to go farther and come to terms with the human condition as such, and understand the range and variety of modes of understanding; we need to see the inadequacies both of the scientist's view of nature and of the present humanities.

Second, there can be no solution of the problem of the *Geisteswissenschaften,* Plessner declares, without a general philosophy of man: a "philosophical anthropology." And this is not possible until we have a *philosophy of nature,*

> not . . . in the Kantian sense of a set of principles for the inorganic world, leaving the life sciences to be quieted by a vague set of "as ifs" or "regulative principles," but in the sense of a philosophical examination of the question *what it means to be alive.* (AB, p. 65)

Dilthey, it is true, in his descriptive psychology, fixed the attention on lived experience *(Erlebnis),* but his thought, as Tillman says,

> was to be increasingly turned in the direction of a hermeneutical interpretation of the outer matrix of *Erlebnis,* the structures of the sociocultural and historical *Lebenswelt,* to which he saw entry through the analysis of the foundation mode of objectification, linguistic expression. *(JBPS,* p. 128)

Only in his earlier works was he close to Husserl's attempts to remain ever close to the historicity of human lived experience, and the recognition of intentionality. Yet he pointed to the problem examined by Plessner, of how we can break the impasse of the conflict between *Naturwissenschaft* and *Geisteswissenschaft*—leading on to the work of Merleau-Ponty—in *Die Stufen des Organischen und der Mensch* of 1928 reissued in 1965. But it is important to recognize that Dilthey "played no small part in Husserl's developing insights into the temporal dimension of consciousness and the typicalities of the life-world," as Tillman declares. Undoubtedly, if we read, say, Medard Boss or R. D. Laing we are reaping the rewards of Dilthey's contributions to the overthrow of positivism, and the disciplines of the understanding of consciousness.

Two further important figures in the development of the phenomenological movement are Max Scheler (1874–1928) and Martin Heidegger (1889–1975). Scheler was concerned to develop a philosophical anthropology along personalistic lines. He sought to develop a positive phenomenology of the emotions as a basis for an ethics. One of his studies was of sympathy, and he sought to make a case for the direct perception of other selves. He is largely remembered as an important influence on later thinkers, especially Helmuth Plessner, Von Weizsacker, and F. J. J. Buytendijk. His works in English include *The Nature of Sympathy* (New Haven: Yale University Press, 1959) *Ressentiment* (New York: Free Press, 1971), *On the Eternal in Man* (London, SCN Press, 1960), and *Man's Place in Nature,* (Boston: Beacon Press, 1961).

Heidegger was a philosopher, of course, and not concerned with psychiatry. According to Speigelberg, he has had an effect on psychotherapy only by accident, as a side issue, though he himself took an interest later in his life in the work of Victor Frankl and Medard Boss. It was a misinterpretation of *Zein und Seit* that contributed to the founding of French existentialism, and led to Ludwig Binswanger's *Daseinsanalyse*, which is the basis of a whole school of existentialist psychotherapy.

But Heidegger began by charging psychology with neglect of its ontological foundations; it fails to explore the mode of being basic for psychological phenomena.

Heidegger's phenomenology had as its main function the interpretation or unveiling of the meaning, often the hidden meaning, of "the phenomenological," as distinguished from the "vulgar" phenomenon, and how it is related to Being. What is difficult to swallow in Heidegger is his rejection of "all that is ordinary." If we take an *ad hominem* point of view, this seems an expression of "schizoid superiority." But he brings psychology and philosophy into the cosmic pattern, as by involving such concepts as Being, *Dasein*, world, time, and death. Man and his psyche are placed before a vast background, so that these questions are offered: How does man relate himself to Being? What is his world and his place in its? How does he experience time?

Dasein is being-in-the-world. Analysis of moods *(Stimmungen)* can be revealing clues to the modes of being *(Seinsweisen)* of Dasein. In this connection Heidegger explored fear *(Furcht)*. In our everyday life *Dasein* can "fall away" *(Verfallen);* other concepts he offered were *Angst* (anxiety) and *Sorge* (concern), in relation to nothingness. All these concepts have been of enormous value to psychotherapy (cf. for example the work of Ludwig Binswanger and Medard Boss) and they have generated a kind of approach that seemed to me useful in understanding, say, the existential problems behind certain forms of modern art, such as Mahler's music and the universal problems of tragedy in literature. Heidegger's most famous works are the 1962 *Being and Time* and the 1949 *What is Metaphysic?* published as *Existence and Being.* (A useful first introduction is Marjorie Grene's *Martin Heidegger,* [London: Bowes and Bowes, 1957]. She studied with Heidegger in Germany.)

Another major figure who must be placed in his historical context in this initial summary of the development of philosophical anthropology is F. J. J. Buytendijk (b. 1887). His personal approach to phenomenology was derived from Max Scheler after 1920. At Scheler's request, Buytendijk visited Cologne between 1920 and 1923, to give lectures there.

Buytendijk does not seem, however, to have made any personal contact with Edmund Husserl, though he has found Husserl's work increasingly significant, and he did hear him lecture in Amsterdam in 1928. In 1948 and in 1956 he delivered lectures himself on the importance of Husserl's work in breaking the stranglehold of Cartesian dualism over psychology and by his return to consciousness as the mode of human subjectivity. Buytendijk

interpreted the call "to the things themselves," says Spiegelberg, as imply-
ing both an unprejudiced nonmetaphysical investigation of immediate
experience, and an attitude of "standing back" (Distanz) for the study of
meaning structures. By exposing the limitations of natural science, Husserl had liberated psychology and the Geisteswissenschaften. Buytendijk
saw what was needed was the attempt to understand what had previously
only been described as "explained." A new kind of understanding was to
be obtained through Wesensschau.[5]

Other influences on Buytendijk's thought were Heidegger, especially his
concept of Dasein, and Gabriel Marcel. He is greatly interested in Sartre,
but rejects him, and he is also interested in Simone de Beauvoir, but
disagrees with her interpretation of the phenomena of the "second sex."[6]
His greatest affinity is with Merleau-Ponty, with whom he had many
common interests; in his book Woman, for instance, he quotes him fre-
quently.

Buytendijk started out as a biologist, and was interested in the psychology of animals. "Life is and remains a mystery," he said. Thus he is a
biologist with a difference. His quest is to understand human existence in
the context of animal life, in the great tradition of German philosophical
anthropology, which displays "unconditional love for everything that
bears the human face." Besides his interest in religion, he has a great
feeling for la joie d'existence and has even written a book on football.

His major works are: Psychologie des animaux (1928); The Mind of the
Dog (1935); Pain: Its Modes and Functions (1962); Woman (1965). A
useful study of his work is made in Marjorie Grene's Approaches to a
Philosophical Biology.

Another major figure in philosophical biology is Kurt Goldstein (1878–
1965). Goldstein is also discussed in Marjorie Grene's Approaches to a
Philosophical Biology and in Herbert Spiegelberg's Phenomenology in
Psychology and Psychiatry. It is interesting to note that Rollo May made
contact with Goldstein and Paul Tillich when they were refugees from
Germany after 1933. Goldstein told May about his organismic theory and
his idea of self-actualization (obviously a powerful influence on May's
existentialism) and with his view of anxiety as a catastrophic reaction of
the organism. This influence, combined with Tillich's existentialism, led
Rollo May to Binswanger's phenomenology and Daseinanalysis. Goldstein's concept of self-actualization lies also behind Abraham Maslow's
psychology and his concept of "peak experiences," those transcendent
moments of being which are the outcome of becoming. Goldstein's main
work, Der Aufbau des Organismus, was included in translation in the
Bibliothèque de Philosophie series of phenomenological works edited by
Merleau-Ponty and Sartre, immediately between Paul Ricoeur's translation of Husserl's Ideen and Heidegger's book on Kant. Spiegelberg sug-

gests that it must have been Merleau-Ponty who initiated this. Spiegelberg seems oddly grudging about admitting Goldstein to the Phenomenology movement, but this does not concern us here, because we are not interested in any kind of philosophical purity. Goldstein said in 1957 that his concept of "existence" was "based on phenomenological observations."

What is perhaps important for present purposes is that Goldstein's philosophy sprang directly from his experience in medicine, and especially from work with brain-damaged patients from World War I. Marjorie Grene says that his work has been too little heeded by English-speaking readers. He has been influential among existentialist psychotherapists, but his general theory of biological knowledge remains largely unknown. In Europe, however, his influence is evident in Merleau-Ponty, in Georges Canquilhem, *La Connaissance de la vie* (1966) and *Le Normal de la pathologique* (1967).

Goldstein worked with Adhemar Gelb (1887–1936) on brain pathology and this work was studied by Scheler, whose late views on philosophical anthropology are discussed in Goldstein's work.[7]

Goldstein also refers to Heidegger and Sartre in his major work, *The Organism,* and he refers to him in an important essay on *The Smile of the Infant* in the festschrift for F. J. J. Buytendijk, *Rencontre, Encounter, Begegnung: Contributions toward a Human Psychology.*[8] In his preface to the second edition of *Der Aufbau des Organismus* in German he discusses the phenomenological-ontological analysis of our understanding of others quoting Binswanger on Heidegger with approval, and quoting from *Sein und Zeit.*

This in Spiegelberg's historical outline of Goldstein's place, we have him linked with Husserl, Scheler, Tillich, Binswanger, Maslow, Merleau-Ponty, Sartre, Heidegger, F. J. J. Buytendijk and others. Marjorie Grene declares "Goldstein's lifetime of experience can hardly be summarised," and he is one of the four Continental thinkers whose work is now becoming known to British psychologists.

Goldstein became aware from brain-damaged patients (with whom he worked from 1905 to 1950) that what could be lost was the "total capacity to handle an environment" by loss of "the abstract attitude." Surprising as it is to the layman, brain damage is crippling because what is lost is the capacity to *abstract,* to hold in the mind, as it were, a whole sense of one's relationship to the world. His emphasis is always on this *wholeness,* and his emphasis is quite away from particulate approaches.[9]

Goldstein found that empirical neurology was unhelpful with the kind of case he was studying, hence he sought a more flexible and comprehensive empiricism. In the case of mental defects he sought "a careful description of the present condition of the organism in which the answer [to a researcher's question] appears."

From this Goldstein went on to declare in his philosophy of biology that *each organism must always be studied as a whole*. This is a methodological, not a metaphysical assertion. As a physician, or an experimentalist, one must approach the individual with reference to its whole nature, even if what one wants to study is the operation of some special part. He insists on being a physician confronting *this* patient (and in this his essentially phenomenological approach will be clear; see, for instance, the work of Medard Boss). Goldstein used the term *Ganzheitsmethode*, which is translated as *holistic*, though Marjorie Grene suggests that *comprehensive* might be a better word.

From this first (biological) principle, the emphasis on the whole consequences follows. First, what is revealed is a *relative constancy* of the whole organism's achievements in its interaction with the environment. A constant pattern is maintained by a living organism, whatever happens to it partially or locally. The interaction of organism and environment geared to a constant mean Goldstein calls the basic law of biology: *das biologische Grundgesetz*.

The constancy of overall performance represents a *preferred* behavior, either of the species or of the individual. Some birds like to fly to South Africa for the winter; and as we know from our own pets and children, each living organism *prefers* to behave in such and such a way—which transcends mere appetite, or "response to stimulus" (indeed the holistic concepts of Goldstein make stimulus-response theory seem quite inadequate). The orientation of behavior toward a preferred performance shows why biology can never be wholly quantitative, why some reference to a qualitative aspect is essential, as of "the best expression of this organism's essential nature" (Grene).

Goldstein even sees the smiling of the infant as an expression of behavior that is both "species-specific" and also more personal, representing the first truly individual encounter of one human being with another, which will deepen into such richness of encounter as each person may attain. *Preferred behavior is that achievement which best expressed the nature of the individual* (Grene, p. 233).[10]

The cultural relevance of such studies, and their importance of English and the humanities, should be evident. Here is a contribution from philosophical biology to perennial philosophical problems. Is it possible to "find" the "other"? Is human meeting ever possible?

Studies in *biology* that attend to signs and meanings find "meeting" a reality, and so redeem the world, because love becomes a principle of life. It finds that aspects of the world make our place in it more meaningful, and it increases our hopes that our own self-realization may be enhanced by *liebende Wirheit:* "the first true encounter of one human being with another, which will deepen uniquely in each lifetime to such riches of encounter as each person may attain" (*AB*, p. 228).

Goldstein's kind of emphasis (on exploring "the best expression of this organism's essential nature") also provides a challenge to established positivistic approaches. The experimentalist supposes himself to be working purely empirically in terms of isolated stimuli and isolated responses. He supposes he has no overall theoretical concept that would distort his purely factual results. Goldstein "weights" in favor of the "whole."

> Goldstein, looking at whatever data may appear relevant in a given situation, is weighting after the fact whatever features of a given performance and of a given individual's repeated or altered performance in a given or altered environment appear, in the light of the whole picture, to have a genuine bearing on that individual's essential character. (*AB*, p. 229)

This approach to the assertion by an individual of his essential character may be related to biological theory. Evolutionary theory makes survival a primary principle. Goldstein demotes survival to a manifestation of disease: his brain-damaged patients were anxiously concerned to hold their world together by whatever means. Goldstein's world is one in which the species and the individual are impelled to enjoy their preferred activity.

If we reduce biology to an atomistic level, all one is aware of is the self-perpetuation of the constituent particulars. Where is there a place for "striving," for "showing of the self on the surface," for the fulfillment of the essential character of the bird or man? Would the Arctic tern really go from one end of the earth to the other for mere survival? A living thing (says Marjorie Grene) exhibits to the naturalist not only "self maintenance" but "comprehensive features of appearance and achievement which constitute the entity whose emergence and whose maintenance such devices as these of inheritance or homeostasis subserve" (*AB*, p. 235).

Here, evidently, Goldstein urges implicity a radical reconsideration of Darwinism: an organism does not adapt so much as seek to be *adequate,* in its "preferred behavior." Marjorie Grene refers to a French biologist, A. Vandel (*L'Homme et l'evolution,* 1958), who argues that we should admit to our place at the pinnacle of evolutionary development, that is, as the species that has achieved the highest degree of individual psychic development on this planet. From this position we can reflect on the conditions that may have led from other less reflective forms of life to our own. His view and Portmann's are reconcilable with evolutionary views, but Goldstein actually displays a positive antipathy to these. He points out, for example, that there is an absolutely basic idea that guides us in evolutionary thinking—that the imperfect becomes intelligible as a variation of the perfect and that the converse is never possible. Marjorie Grene is doubtful of Goldstein's reaction to Darwinism, but as some have pointed out, evolutionary theory does rest on negative processes, and belongs to the nineteenth century and its devil-take-the-hindmost social thinking and metaphysical pessimism.[11]

The questioning of evolutionary theory, however, is peripheral to Goldstein's own concerns. He is concerned, as a neurologist, to refute the interpretation of behavior in terms of reflexology. This links him with Erwin Straus, who has rejected Pavlov, and with Buytendijk and Plessner, who have also written against conditioned-reflex theory. Goldstein argues that "reflexes" belong to distorted and isolated parts of organisms, not to the living whole. An organism that is studied in reflexological terms is like one of his brain-damaged patients who can only live in the rigid routine of the war veteran's hospital.

Second, a point that reinforces Straus, the situation studied by the reflexologist is distorted and artificial; it is not found in nature, where a more spontaneous kind of behavior is usually found. Reflexes are more common in higher than in lower animals; taken in context, a reflex is nothing but "the simplest reaction of living substance as such" (*Aufbau*, p. 115). It is not true that complex behavior is simply made up of these simple units: the data, Goldstein argues, tend to refute rather than support reflex theory.

Conditioned reflexes characterize only higher organisms—and chiefly man. Pavlov's experiments fail to show us whether the natural environment of the dog would ever present conditions suitable for the formation of such reflexes. It is only through man's interference that they occur! Do the experiments on animals in laboratories do any more than show how animal behavior can be distorted by human experimenters?[12] Besides *The Organism,* Goldstein's most important work is *Human Nature in the Light of Psychopathology.*[13]

Adolf Portmann has been mentioned. He too is a biologist with a difference. He opposes reductionist biology, which seeks to reduce everything to its psychochemical base, a new philosophy of living things, to guide the biologist's understanding of his world. The work of Portmann's to begin with, is *New Paths in Biology*. By his concept of centricity and its emphasis on the intrinsic value of the entities in the world of life, Portmann helps to rescue us in yet another way from the naturalistic, one-level world. Marjorie Grene relates some of his concepts to Goldstein's thought. Portmann discusses *Innerlichkeit* ("inwardness") as a pervasive characteristic of life. He is interested in "display" *(Selbstdarstellung)* and "centricity," also "relation to the environment through inwardness" *(Weltbeziehung durch Innerlichkeit)*. Such concepts oblige the biologist to try to understand living things by trying to "feel how their way of living feels" (Marjorie Grene), and this redeems the universe by indicating our involvement with it in knowing. Here, again, is indwelling as the basis of knowing.

Portmann's major works are *Animals as Social Beings, New Paths in Biology, Animal Forms and Patterns, Animal Camouflage*, and "Time in the Life of the Organism." Marjorie Grene offers an account of his work in *Approaches to a Philosophical Biology* (pp. 2–54). From animal biology we turn to psychotherapy with Ludwig Binswanger (1881–1966). A proponent of phenomenology, he also devised *Daseinsanalyse* or *Dasein*-analysis, an approach to psychotherapy based on Heidegger's philosophy. He was born into a German family that moved to Switzerland, and that had been involved in psychiatry. His grandfather had founded the Bellevue Sanatorium in Kreuzlingen. He studied medicine and served his internship with Eugen Bleuler at Burghölzli, Zurich. He worked with C. G. Jung, who introduced him to Freud. Max Scheler, Heidegger, Ernest Cassirer, and Martin Buber all came to visit his sanitorium, which became an international meeting ground for those interested in new approaches to therapy. Most of his important essays are publishes in *Being-in-the-World*, ed. Jacob Needleman.

Other important essays to read in getting a grasp of this historical movement are in *Existence—A New Dimension in Psychiatry*, ed. Rollo May, Ernest Angel, Henri F. Ellenberger, especially the first two chapters. See also "Existential Analysis and Psychotherapy," *Psychoanalytical Review* 45 (1958–59): 19–83. Binswanger, as we have seen, picks up themes from Heidegger's *Sein und Zeit*, which was published in 1927 and also influenced the philosophical anthropology of Viktor von Gebsattel and Erwin Straus. In 1930 a new journal was launched, *Nervenarzt*, which was an outlet for the new phenomenological anthropology.

Binswanger broke down the boundaries of Jasper's phenomenology. This had confined itself to describing isolated subjective phenomena characteristic of the psychotic patient. He extended this approach to make a study of the subjective life-history of a patient, and to describe the connections between successive elements of phenomenal experience. Jaspers thought schizophrenia unintelligible in principle. Binswanger tried to understand it, using Heidegger's analytic of human *Dasein*. Binswanger sought to develop a full-fledged philosophical anthropology, says Herbert Spiegelberg, based on Heidegger's conception of *Dasein* as being-in-the-world.

In this he was supported by von Gebsattel, Eugene Minkowski, and Straus. Von Gebsattel was much influenced by Scheler, who was a philosophical anthropologist. Straus was reacting against Pavlov and the conception of man as a mechanism operating by reflexes. He sought to restore the unity of man in the face of Descartes' dualism, which he saw as leading inevitably to Pavlovian behaviorism; phenomenology was to be the means to capture this unity. In France Eugene Minkowski was following much the same path.

A great deal of Binswanger's work has yet to be translated.[14] This thinker's rejection of Sartre is important.[15] He is also discussed in Marjorie Grene, *Approaches to a Philosophical Biology* (pp. 166, 195).

We have seen that Martin Heidegger took note of another important figure in the development of existential psychotherapy, Viktor Frankl (1905–75). Frankl became professor of psychiatry and neurology at the University of Vienna and head of the department of neurology at the Vienna Poliklinik. He was the founder of "logotherapy," on which he published various books, a form of therapy based on *meaning*.

In *Psychotherapy and Existentialism* he states his underlying philosophy of life in the form of three assumptions (1) freedom of will, (2) the will of meaning, (3) the meaning of life, for which he claimed phenomenological support. His impulse was to find an alternative to Freud's psychology, based on the will to pleasure, and to Adler's, based on the will to power. He defined his approach as *Existenzanalyse* and *Logotherapie*, but Spiegelberg believes his approach has little to do with Binswanger's *Daseinsanalyse* or Boss's *Daseinanalytic*. Frankl's aim was more therapeutic than theoretical, and concerned itself with psychological problems arising from the "existential vacuum" or "existential frustration," and the resultant spiritual or "noogenic" neurosis.

Frankl's approach to psychotherapy was devised from his experiences during several years in Nazi concentration camps, where he lost his entire family, but managed to construct a book which was taken from him and destroyed.[16]

As Spiegelberg says, Frankl is not one of the major practitioners of phenomenology, nor is phenomenology a major point of his work. But it has helped him to move beyond Freud and Adler, the two great previous proponents of individual psychology in Vienna. He has indicated how phenomenology could be applied more critically to work in psychotherapy.

A whole historical stream, of course, is the transition of ideas derived from phenomenology to America, not least by the emigration of certain leading figures who were refugees from Nazism. Erwin Straus (1891–1975) was one of the most important figures here. Binswanger considered him the cleverest of the original circle of phenomenological anthropologists.

He went to the United States in 1939 and from then on has established an international reputation. He finally settled down at the Veterans Hospital, Lexington, Kentucky and began to establish there an intellectual center for phenomenology in the New World.

Straus started from and always returned to psychiatry. He believed like Maslow that in order to understand the abnormal it is necessary to study the norm, a task that required more than "science" could supply. He sought an understanding of the *conditio humana,* says Spiegelberg, the

Psychologie der menschlichen Welt. This is the task of phenomenological psychology.

Straus, too, attended some of Scheler's lectures. He was, however, doubtful of Husserl because, as an anti-Pavlovian psychologist, he felt that Husserl was too attached to Descartes. Straus's attack on Pavlov was itself condemned as anti-scientific, and this debate was the beginning of his first major work, *Vonn Sinn der Sinne* (1935), translated as *The Primary World of Senses* (1963).

Later, Straus made contact with Binswanger; he had already been in touch with Minkowski and von Gebsattel. Binswanger and Straus disagreed over Straus's theories of *Erlebnis* (lived experience), and Straus felt fundamental disagreements with Binswanger over the concept of *Dasein* from Heidegger.

At this moment the Nazi conquest disrupted Straus's work as a neurologist and psychiatrist in Berlin, and he fled to America, teaching psychology at first at Black Mountain College.

His work, which is discussed by Marjorie Grene in *Approaches,* may be summed up by his delineation of his own project:

> In my own work I have tried to "save" sensory experience from theoretical misinterpretation and then to apply the regained understanding of the norm to pathological manifestations.

Straus's major works, besides *The Primary World of Senses,* are *On Obsession: A Clinical and Methodological Study,* Nervous and Mental Disease monographs; *Psychiatry and Philosophy;* and *Phenomenological Psychology: Selected Papers.*

Goldstein, Paul Tillich and Erwin Straus have been influential, as refugee scholars, on one of the most influential authorities on existential phenomenology in America, Rollo May (b. 1907) Straus asked May to speak on "The Phenomenological Bases of Psychotherapy" at the first Lexington Conference on Phenomenology in 1964 *(Phenomenology: Pure and Applied).*

May began his early adulthood as an artist in Europe and has never abandoned his interest in artistic creativity. In the thirties he began his psychological work as a counselor, and wrote *The Meaning of Anxiety* (1950).

His next work is *Man's Search for Himself* (1953), a preexistentialist attempt to deal with problems of the loss of the sense of self in our time, the loss of the sense of tragedy. His solution is the rediscovery of selfhood, culminating in creative self-consciousness. From 1950 to 1954 he seems to have moved more deeply into European existentialist thought, and *Existence—A New Dimension in Psychiatry* was published in 1958, under a joint editorship with Ernest Angel and Henri F. Ellenberger. Ernest Angel was apparently (according to Spiegelberg) the initiator of this symposium, a psychologist and co-editor at Basic Books. Paul Tillich was also consulted.

In 1961 May published *Psychology and the Human Dilemma* and in 1969, *Love and Will.* His work has generated a whole new movement in existentialism and phenomenology in America. His work is intellectually exacting, and his message is by no means easy or comfortable, yet he is a best-seller in America. (In Great Britain, by contrast, his publisher had to take a half-page advertisement in *The Times,* to ask, "Why this conspiracy of silence?" *Love and Will* was not reviewed anywhere, presumably because it criticized "enlightenment" and "permissive" assumptions, and expressed doubts about standard progressivism.)

The *Journal of Existential Psychiatry* was started in 1960 by Jordan Scher in Chicago. In 1964 it was converted into a more philosophical *Journal of Existentialism,* under new editors, while Scher started another journal, *Existential Psychiatry,* in 1966. In 1959 was launched the American Association for Existential Psychology and Psychiatry, and in 1961 *The Review of Existential Psychology and Psychiatry.* In all these journals Viktor Frankl, Minkowski, Binswanger, Medard Boss, Paul Tillich, F. J. J. Buytendijk, Marcel, Helmuth Plessner, and Carl Rogers published articles, while the proceedings of a 1959 Conference in New York were published as *Existential Psychology.*

Abraham Maslow contributed to a new movement seeking an alternative to behaviorism and psychoanalysis, which he called "Third Force Psychology," and he led a new movement called "Humanistic Psychology" that published a journal called the *Journal of Humanistic Psychology.* In this, existentialist psychology was one stream, though in *Challenges of Humanistic Psychology,* edited by Bugental in 1967, the only phenomenological contribution was by Colin Wilson on Husserl.

Bugental (who wrote *The Search for Authenticity*) attempted to combine a humanistic psychology with existentialism. He, like Rollo May, stressed the tragic side of human existence, and emphasizes the need for meaning and "validation." His central stress is an "awareness" that seems to mean being-in-the-world in accord with the "givenness" of man's nature and the world.

Abraham Maslow's 1962 *Towards a Psychology of Being* is important because he declares that too much in psychology and psychiatry has been developed from abnormal people who were incapable of joy, transcendence, and meaning—what he calls "peak experiences." Maslow also saw that in the more creative forms of existentialism and phenomenology there were emerging new models of man, and new concepts of value.

Maslow's most important emphasis is on the moral implications of the rediscovery of the intentional, and of the primacy of man's pursuit of meaning. He speaks of

> a clear confrontation of one basic set of values by another never system of values which claims to be not only more efficient but more true. It draws on some of the truly revolutionary consequences of the discovery that human nature has been sold short, that man has a higher nature which is just as 'instinctoid' as his lower nature and that this higher nature includes the need for meaningful work, for responsibility, for creativeness, for being fair and just for doing what is worthwhile and for preferring to do it well. (*Towards a Philosophy of Being,* p. 122)

"Reduction to the concrete is a loss of future" he says, speaking of the predicament of certain patients; but he is also evidently aware that this may be seen as a general statement about our kind of society, in its imprisonment in "objective" or naturalistic concepts of man's make-up.

Other important recent figures in American existentialist and phenomenological thinking are Joseph Lyons, *Psychology and the Measure of Man* (1963): Adrian Van Kaam, *Existential Foundations of Psychology* (1966); and Herbert Spiegelberg, in his two masterly surveys of the whole philosophical movement, *Phenomenology in Psychology and Psychiatry* (1972), and, on a wider canvas, *The Phenomenological Movement* (1965).

Another figure who has a place in the philosophical movement is Eugene Minkowski, who was born in Poland in 1895. Minkowski studied at Warsaw and Munich. In 1910 he received a medical diploma at Kazan in Russia, and then went to study philosophy in Germany. When war broke out in 1914 he escaped to Switzerland and joined Eugen Bleuler at Burgholzli, the psychiatric university hospital. After a period in the French Army he practiced in Paris for many years as a psychiatrist, being a director of the *Foyer des Soulins,* an institution for children with character disorders.

Minkowski began as a medical biologist, but became increasingly interested in psychology and philosophy, under the influence of Bergson and Husserl. He has been a member of the Commission and Medical Superior Committee for mental patients at the French Ministry of Public Health, and has an honorary medical degree from the University of Zurich.

His publications include *La Schizophrenie* (1926); *Le Temps Vecu* (1933); *Vers un Cosmologie* (1936). He is a pioneer in phenomenological psychoanalysis.

To return to the English scene is to return to one in which all this European-American movement seems to count for very little. The pragmatic, positivist, and analytical nature of our traditions of thought generate a distrust of "reflective" philosophy. R. D. Laing once began to take in his hands the links with Europe when he edited the studies in Existentialism and Phenomenology for the Tavistock Press. This movement seems, however, to have come to naught, except for Laing's important first book, *The Divided Self,* and later *The Self and Others.* Laing also offered valuable suggestions in *Interpersonal Perception: A Theory and Method of Research* (1960), while a new book, *The Voice of Experience,* offers a useful critique of positivism as it is found in psychiatry and psycho-analysis (London: Tavistock, 1982). He also did some interesting work with Aron Esterson, as in *The Leaves of Spring,* about schizophrenic families. However, the history of R. D. Laing is a sad one, characteristic of our time; he became a television guru and a cult figure who gradually ceased to count in serious debate, because of his energetic and wild radicalism, while the series of important books he was editing has now lapsed. There was a strong native movement that could have been linked with this body of work, which included Erwin Straus's *Phenomenological Psychology,* including the writings of Winnicott himself, Masud Khan, Peter Lomas, Harry Guntrip, and W. R. D. Fairbairn. Yet, as so often during the period since the sixties, the interest in new approaches dis-solved into fragmentation, pseudo-radicalism, and futile destructiveness (the slogan of the "Anti-university," which Laing graced for a time, was "Black Power! Madness! Revolution!").

Winnicott's work, however, has now, apparently, reached Paris and has become the focus of intellectual interest, while elsewhere, as in Canada, some like Andrew Brink have made a great deal of serious use of British contributions from writers on psychoanalysis such as Melanie Klein, Winnicott, Fairbairn, and Guntrip. However, there seems to have been an absolute decline in general interest in ideas from psychoanalysis, possibly under the influence of those like H. J. Eysenck who have tried to show that psychoanalysis is not respectable because it cannot stand up to positivistic examination of its "cures." (Roger Poole, however, accuses Eysenck of "alchemy" in his methods, which include obtaining answers through questionnaires to complex inner problems, and then putting them through a computer.)

There is little excitement about the genuinely phenomenological work of writers like Marion Milner and Marie Naevestad, while theoretical theories like those of Jacques Lacan seem popular among the young, who pursue them along with equally abstract theories from lingistics. Yet in Lacan the model of human nature and the metapsychology seem to be based on a largely outdated Freudianism, long since displaced by post-Freudian thought, as delineated in Guntrip's excellent critical histories, *Personality Structure and Human Interaction* and *Schizoid Phenomena, Object-Relations and the Self.*

Marion Milner's work is essentially phenomenological, especially *In the Hands of the Living God* (1969): and there is also *Existential Neurosis* by

E. K. Ledermann (1972), a book that is discussed below. The relevance of these studies in psychotherapy does not, however, yet seem to be recognized by the British Society for Phenomenology; the work of drawing on this immense revolution seems simply not yet begun in Britain. Yet, I believe, we must persist in trying to draw attention to it. By contrast with traditional "scientific" psychology and even Freudian psychology, it brings to the center of the human picture man's cultural life and achievements, and thus questions of meaning and values. Its spheres of attention are consciousness and subjective experience, and so, where education is concerned, it offers us a more complex, whole, and more satisfactory account of what knowing is. And so, too, it embraces as a humanities discipline the present crisis of human existence.

The present writer is not qualified to delineate what has been happening in established philosophy, except to say that students who seek in the study of philosophy some engagement with the problems of being do not seem to find it.

As Gabriel Marcel declares, in his *Tragic Wisdom and Beyond* (1973), philosophy can be supported only if it involves an actual responsibility in the face of the unprecedented crisis confronting man at the moment. The deadness of present-day philosophy seems disastrous in the light of this. As Marcel reported, "When I was at the Lima conference in 1951 I spoke with A. J. Ayer about a 'philosophy of reflection' ": these words, Marcel found, which in France designated an incontestably venerable tradition, were meaningless to Ayer.[17] At Harvard, Marcel found that many philosophy professors were discouraging students "from looking for a relation between the most exclusive analytical thought in which they were being trained and life . . . the problems that life poses to each one of us but which seemed in the professors' eye to be merely matters for personal discretion" (Ibid., p. 17). While philosophy remains in academic centers a kind of intellectual game, a limbering-up exercise for the mind, and while philosophy and psychology claim that kind of abstract detachment, they cannot be justified at a time when "our life is threatened at every level."

This situation is the focus of dismay and concern on the part of one English lecturer in Britain, who has also had training in philosophy and has written a thesis on Kierkegaard, Roger Poole. Poole has made his position clear not only in his book *Towards Deep Subjectivity,* discussed below, but also in some substantial articles, namely, "Modern Masters of Philosophy"; *Books and Bookmen* (August 1975) and "From Phenomenology to Subjective Method," in *Universities Quarterly* 29, no. 4 (Autumn 1975): 412.

One further source of understanding may be mentioned—straightforward anthropology, such as we find in Richard Leakey's *Origins.* Leakey's is an important book because he reveals the inadequacies of the "scientific" view of man offered by such popular writers as Robert Ardrey, Desmond Morris, and even Konrad Lorenz. There have, of course, been previous replies to the "naked ape" myth, for example, *Naked Ape—or Homo Sapiens?* by Bernard Towers and John Lewis.[18] These authors accused Desmond Morris of being scientifically inaccurate in many ways. But Leakey and his co-author base their rejection of the "naked ape" myth on many years of study of the extremely ancient remains of hominids in the cradle of man's existence, Africa. What they find, briefly, is that there is no evidence in these remains that man is basically aggressive or brutal, by genetic endowment or instinct. On the contrary, every indication is that man evolved to his higher state because he is "cooperation man." The crushed skulls and so forth on which the present myths have been constructed came to be that way because of natural causes, the collapse of caves, or other phenomena, and not by conflict at all.

Lorenz, one of the founders of modern ethology, actually wrote, "There is evidence that the first inventors of pebble tools—the African australopithecines—promptly used their weapons to kill game, but fellow members of their own species as well" (*On Aggression,* p. 37). The main burden of Lorenz's book was that "the human species carries with it an inescapable legacy of territoriality and aggression, instincts which must be ventilated lest they spill over in ugly fashion." In this approach to the nature of man's nature and existence, archaeological evidence, says Leakey, was brought to weave and form *"one of the most dangerously persuasive myths of our time: that man is incorrigibly belligerent: that war and violence are in our genes."* As Leakey says, this view was assimilated with unseemly haste into a popular conventional wisdom—enhanced by the elegant prose of Desmond Morris and the work of Robert Ardrey. Leakey and Roger Lewin reject this conventional "wisdom" on three *(scientific)* grounds. First, no theory of human nature can be so firmly proved. Second, much of the "evidence" used to erect this theory is simply not relevant to human behavior. Third, such clues as there are from science suggest that man is essentially cooperative. To make these points is not to deny the existence of aggression as a human problem. But, as the authors show in the rest of their book, human nature and behaving are so complex that the simplifications of the "aggression" and "naked ape" myths are ridiculous. Our nearest relations in the animal world—for example, gorillas and chimpanzees—are nonterritorial. And when it comes to human acts like cannibalism, these may be done not for reasons of aggression at all, but actually because of a symbolic need to establish a sense of continuity. In the animal kingdom the management of conflict is largely through mock battles. But farther along the evolutionary path, carrying out the appropriate avoidance behavior comes to depend more and more on learning, and in social animals the channel of learning is social education. And, as the pictures of babies at their mother's breasts imply in Leakey's book, an important element in human behavior is *"liebende Wirheit"*—"loving communion," a concept that is, of course, preeminent in the philosophical anthropology delineated here.

Aggression is no inbuilt element in the animal kingdom. Human beings are not innately disposed powerfully either to aggression or to peace. In the evolutionary picture, surely, an innate drive for killing individuals of one's own species would soon have wiped that species out. And then Leakey makes an important statement:

> Humans, as we know, did not blunder up an evolutionary blind alley, a fate that innate, unrestrained aggressiveness would undoubtedly have produced. (*Origins*, p. 213)

As I have suggested earlier, Leakey remains very much within the orthodoxy of Darwinian evolutionary theory, and lives with the consequent fallacies. But in declaring that human beings did not "blunder up an evolutionary alley" he is, whether he recognizes it or not, pointing to order and an organizing principle of some kind: the statement is not one that endorses the "chance and necessity" view.

The whole skeptical, "natural brute" metaphysic has powerful political influence. But as Leakey himself argues, the result is a deep impulse toward irresponsibility, and avoidance of the real problems: "There are many reasons why a youth may 'spontaneously' smash a window or make an attack on an old lady, but an inborn drive inherited from our animal origins is certainly not one of them. . . . Urban problems will not be solved by pointing to supposed defects in our genes while ignoring real defects in social justice" (p. 223). "Those who argue that war is in our genes not only are wrong, but they also *commit the crime of diverting attention from the real causes of war*" (ibid., emphasis added).

Leakey's is a deeply stimulating book, and it cannot be fully summarized here. His conclusions are marvelously positive. "We are essentially cultural animals with the capacity to formulate many kinds of social structures; but a deep-seated biological urge towards cooperation, towards working as a group, provides a basic framework for those structures."

At the end Leakey reverts to conventional evolutionary theory, and persists in attributing our origins to "accident." At the same time, however, he warns us that our future is in our own hands; our predicament cannot, therefore, be determined by any "natural laws" or "instincts" but is an aspect of our freedom. "To have arrived on this earth as the product of biological accident, only to depart through human arrogance, would be the ultimate irony." (p. 256). This provides a valuable emphasis. But, of course, the problem becomes ever more exacting if we see our development not as a mere "accident," but as the product of a perpetual urge of matter, of the universe, to become conscious of itself. I leave for discussion elsewhere the problem of the need to resist the implicit metaphysic in mechanistic Darwinism and its descendants. It is by no means proven, as many scientists seem to believe, that life came into existence by "accident" and that the multitudinous forms of life owe their existence only to "chance and necessity." These are hypotheses, not "facts." Consciousness, declares E. W. F. Tomlin, cannot be believed to have come into existence by accident. To examine the dreadful, but enthralling, problems that now arise, in answer to the question, "What is it to be Human?" we now need to marry the humanistic disciplines of a Leakey (who is well aware of the nature of man as *animal symbolicum*)— that is, archaeology, paleoanthropology, primatology, anthropology, and geology—with the new disciplines of philosophical anthropology—as in the work of those whom Marjorie Grene interprets for us, in phenomenology, psychoanalysis, and the holistic studies of man and his meaning. In this, poetry has its place, and the analysis of culture on phenomenological lines—that is, by the analysis of the meanings of consciousness. Insofar as students of man's nature can escape from an inadequate approach that remains rooted in nineteenth-century natural science, in physicalism, and in positivism, and dare to encounter the baffling concept and disciplines to which Marjorie Grene and others are pointing, we may look forward to a new and positive sense of man's role, his creative nature, and his achievements, which could certainly have enormous implications for education and the humanities.

Notes

1. See Anton C. Rancurelto, *A Study of Franz Brentano: His Psychological Standpoint and His Significance in the History of Psychology* (New York: Academic Press, 1968). Also Karl Stumpf, "Selbstdarstellung," in *History of Psychology in Autobiography*, ed. Carl Murchison (Worcester, Mass.: Clark University Press, 1930), pp. 389–441, a lucid and interesting account of his position.

2. W. Dilthey, *Gesammelte Schriften* (Berlin: Leipniz and Bolin, 1914–36), 7:213–16. Translated into English as *Wilhelm Dilthey* by H. A. Hodges (New York: Oxford University Press, 1944), pp. 121–24. T. Lipps, *Asthetik* (Hamburg: Leopold Voss, 1903).

3. One of Dilthey's pupils, Bernhard Groethuysen, has given an excellent description of the development of anthropological philosophy in "Philosophische Anthropologie," *Handbuch der Philosophie* (Munich and Berlin: Reichl, 1931), 3:1–207. Se also "Towards an Anthropological Philosophy," in *Philosophy and History Essays Presented to Ernst Cassirer* (Oxford: Clarendon Press, 1936), pp. 77–89.

4. Edmund Husserl, *Phenomenology and the Crisis of Philosophy*, trans. Quentin Lauer, S. J. (New York: Harper and Rowe, 1965), pp. 187–88.

5. See Buytendijk, "The Significance of Husserl's Phenomenology for Present Psychol-

ogy," in *Husserl et la Pensée moderne, Phaenomenologica* 2 (1959): 78–98. *Wesensschau* is a term from Husserl meaning essential insight or intuiting.

6. There is a valuable discussion of Simone de Beauvoir's attitude to woman from a phenomenological point of view in Karl Stern, *The Flight from Woman*.

7. See Kurt Goldstein, *The Organism: A Holistic Approach to Biology Derived from Pathological Data in Man*, foreword by K. Lashley (New York: American Books, 1939; paperback ed. Beacon Press, 1964).

8. The festschrift was published by Spectrum in Utrecht in 1957.

9. See "Kurt Goldstein" in B. G. Boring and A. Lindsey, eds., *History of Psychology in Autobiography* (New York: Appleton-Century-Crofts, 1967), vol. 5. See also B. Rimbaud, *Infantile Autism* (New York: Appleton-Century-Crofts, 1964). Goldstein's work does seem relevant to the perplexing problem of autistic phenomena.

10. See Kurt Goldstein, "The Smiling of the Infant and the Problem of Understanding the "Other," *Journal of Psychology* 44 (1957): 175–91. In this Goldstein closely follows Buytendijk's and Plessner's studies.

11. See Norman Macbeth, *Darwin Retried* (London: Garnstone, 1976), also E. W. F. Tomlin, "Fallacies of Evolutionary Theory," in *The Encyclopaedia of Ignorance*, ed. Ronald Duncan and Miranda Weston-Smith (Oxford: Pergamon, 1977). See also *Evolution and the Humanities*, by the present author, Aldershot, Gower Press, 1987.

12. This theme has been more recently taken up by W. H. Thorpe in *Nature and Human Nature*, who argues that scientists can turn animals into morons. See also Erwin Straus, *The Primary World of Senses*, and Mary Midgeley, *Beast and Man*.

13. See "Kurt Goldstein" in E. G. Boring and G. Lindsey, eds., *History of Psychology in Autobiography* (New York: Appleton, 1967).

14. The following do not seem to have been translated. *Einführung in die Probleme der allgemeinen Psychologie* (Berlin: Springer, 1922); *Über Ideenflucht* (Zurich: Ovell Fuessli, 1933); *Grundformen und Drkenntnis menschichen Daseins* (Zurich: Niehans, 1942): *Drei formen missglückten Daseins* (Tubingen: Niemeyer, 1956); *Schizophrenie* (Pfullingen: Neske, 1957); *Melancholie und Manie* (Pfullingen: Neske, 1960); *Wahn* (Pfullingen: Neske, 1965). The main sources of information on Binswanger are in *Being-in-the-World*, ed. Jacob Needleman (New York: Basic Books, 1963); *Phenomenology: Pure and Applied*, ed. Erwin Straus (Pittsburgh, Pa: Duquesne University Press, 1964); and *Existence* (New York: Basic Books, 1958). See also *Sigmund Freud, Reminiscences of a Friendship* (1956; New York: Grune and Stratton, 1957).

15. See Henri Ellenberger on Buber's influence on Binswanger in "Binswanger's Existential Analysis," in *Existence—A New Dimension in Psychiatry*, ed. Rollo May et al. (New York: Basic Books, 1958).

16. See *Man's Search for Meaning: From Death-Camp to Existentialism*, trans. Ilse Lasch (Boston: Beacon Press, 1963) and *The Doctor and the Soul*, trans. Richard and Clara Winston (New York: Knopf, 1965). Frankl's books are now published in England by Souvenir Press and some have been in paperback in Penguin Books.

17. Yet Ayer evidently believes that he has solved all the important philosophical questions! As Roger Poole said, reviewing *The Central Questions of Philosophy*, "They are no longer the central questions. . . . *The Central Questions* leaves too much out. . . . Professor Ayer [has] stated that he has come more and more to regard philosophy as the study of *proof.* The study of philosophy in the English speaking world is stagnant. It refuses the urgent historical tasks before it. . . ." *Books and Bookmen*, June 1974, p. 50. As E. W. F. Tomlin points out, A. J. Ayer dismisses as non-sensical not merely the statements of theologians and metaphysicians, but such common statements as "stealing money is wrong." Such a contention, says Tomlin, himself a philosopher, surely belongs to that class of fatuous theory which can only be entertained in the lecture room. See *The Eastern*

Philosophies (London: Hutchinson, 1956), pp. 307–8, and Marjorie Grene on Bertrand Russell: "Russell himself once said in a letter to *The Listener* that so far as philosophy goes—and that means hard-nosed empirical philosophy implemented through extensional logic—there is no difference, so far as he could see, between a dislike of merciless cruelty and a liking for oysters. So Russell the pacifist. Russell the humanitarian lived a life schizophrenically at odds with his philosophy." (Grene, *Philosophy in and out of Europe*, p. 16)

18. See also *Beyond Chance and Necessity*, ed. John Lewis.

5
How Do We Know a Child?

Above I said that we must be ready in the study of man for "meeting."
What does this mean? What is the relationship between "reciprocity" and
learning? What do we mean when we say that unless we "encounter" a
subject in biology, we cannot find what we are looking for? A good example
to take in examining these questions—one of great relevance to education—is how do we investigate the nature of the child?

In a recent psychology book I saw a photograph of a characteristic
"scientific" experiment, intended for the investigation of baby behavior. A
research worker was gazing through a machine at a baby's eye movements
as she presented to him a series of images. The mechanism of the baby's
response had been divided, in a characteristic Cartesian way, from the
whole complex, of feeling, of emotion in relationship. D. W. Winnicott,
pediatrician and psychoanalyst, once started a gathering of therapists by
declaring that there was "such a thing as a baby"; what he meant was that
the baby is always part of a "nursing couple" and really exists only within
the context of psychic parturition, in which the mother's "maternal preoccupation," a schizoid extension of her personality, is crucial to the baby's
development, to its capacities to see the world. Thus, half the existence of
the subject was not there in the above psychological empirical experiment—so it is an example of science's not being able to find the object of
its inquiry. And this is one of the main problems with objective psychology; it cannot find its own subject.

The essence of the subject of inquiry here is evidently *encounter;*
anyone seeking to find this must surely abandon the "objective" position,
which can only take encounter as "one item among others in the indif-
ferent catalogue of spatio temporally perceived objects." These are Marjorie Grene's words, interpreting F. J. J. Buytendijk's statement of his
method. Buytendijk believed that behavior cannot be understood by objective methods. "Encounter, as a form of behavior, is a mode of 'being-in-
the-world,' and as such can only be understood if we share it, if we
ourselves live encounter with others and so approach through participation as well as observation" (*AB*, p. 162).

If the woman scientist in the above-mentioned experiment had been handling the baby, and reacting to its expressions, she might have learned more; and, of course, one essential ingredient would then be her contribution to the encounter: her intuitive response. So in psychology, even the very idea of looking at the object of inquiry has to be reexamined, since we are attending to beings that are to be seen neither as objects, nor even as complete subjects!

If we look at the findings of a child psychotherapist such as D. W. Winnicott, obviously he is employing more than one kind of observation, and is bringing to bear on the question of early development his own (subjective) experience of children, of adult patients in regression, or psychotics, and other clinical experience as well as that of mentally ill children. He is thus able to experience, for example, what it is like to be unintegrated, because he has allowed himself to be confronted with problems in patients for which he has had to enter, virtually, into the mother's responsive role of "being for" an unintegrated infant. Encounters with individuals who are unintegrated, depersonalized, and have no sense of space, time, or reality, have enabled him to see that

a great deal that we take for granted had a beginning and a condition out of which it developed. . . . There are three processes which seem to me to start very early: (1) integration (2) personalization and (3) . . . the appreciation of time and space and other properties of reality, in short, realization. (*CP*, p. 149)

Winnicott knows that in his work he will encounter real people who have real problems in this area:

Another psychotic patient discovered in analysis that most of the time she lived in her head, behind her eyes. She could only see out of her eyes as out of windows and so was not aware of what her feet were doing, and in consequence she tended to fall into pits and trip over things. She had no "eyes in her feet." Her personality was not felt to be localized in her body, which was like a complex engine that she had to drive with conscious care and skill. Another patient, at times, lived in a box 20 yards up, only connected with her body by a slender thread. (*CP*, p. 149)

Being integrated enough to see as if from within one's own body he is able to see, is *an achievement created by the mother's handling:*

The tendency to integrate is helped by two sets of experience: the technique infant care whereby an infant is kept warm, handled and bathed and rocked and named, and also the acute instinctual experiences which tend to gather the personality together from within. . . . There are long stretches of time in a normal infant's life in which a baby does not mind whether he is many bits or one whole being, or whether he lives in his mother's face or in his own body provided that from time to time he comes together and feels something. . . .

> In regard to environment, bits of nursing techniques and faces seen and sounds heard and smells smelt are only gradually pieced together into one being to be called mother. (*CP*, p. 150)

Through such processes the human being comes to find himself and his world, and then to find a meaningful word. Winnicott's account of them is phenomenological.

Winnicott goes on to say "let us assume integration"—and at once follows "another enormous subject—the primary relation to external reality."

> If we allow analysis of psychotics, we find that in some analyses this essential lack of true relation to external reality is almost the whole thing.
> I will try to describe in the simplest possible terms this phenomenon as I see it. In terms of baby and mother's breast (I am not claiming that the breast is essential as a vehicle of mother-love)[1] the baby has instinctual urges and predatory ideas. The mother has a breast and the power to produce milk, and the idea that she would like to be attacked by a hungry baby. These two phenomena do not come into relation with each other till the mother and child *live an experience together*. The mother being mature and physically able has to be the one with tolerance and understanding, so that it is she who produces a situation that may with luck result in the first tie the infant makes with an external object, an object that is external to the self from the infant's point of view.
> I think of the process as if two lines come near each other. If they overlap there is a moment of *illusion*—a bit of experience which the infant can take as *either* his hallucination *or* a thing belonging to external reality. (*CP*, p. 152)

Winnicott goes on to say that, in other language, the infant comes to the breast when excited, and ready to hallucinate something first to be "attacked." At that moment the actual breast appears and he is able to feel it was that nipple that he hallucinated. So his ideas are enriched by actual details of sight, feel, smell, and next this material is "used" in the hallucination. In this way he starts to build up a capacity to conjure up what is actually available. The mother has to go on giving the infant this type of experience. This enables him to have confidence in the world. The process is immensely simplified if the infant is cared for from birth by his own mother, or failing that by the adopted mother, and not by several nurses.

> It is especially at the start that mothers are vitally important, and indeed it is a mother's job to protect her infant from complications that cannot yet be understood by the infant, and to go on steadily providing the simplified bit of the world which the infant, through her, comes to know. Only on such a foundation can objectivity or scientific attitude be built. All failure in objectivity at whatever date relates to failure in this state of primitive emotional development. (*CP*, p. 153)

This, as Winnicott admits, is but the fringe of a vast subject. But is the way in which he discusses it not a "useful explanation"? Or, rather, a useful *understanding?* It is certainly not based on "observables"; but it is based on Husserl's "I-type of being and life." Winnicott is opening up the vast problem of the initial steps in the development of a relation to external reality, and the relation of fantasy to reality. At the start a simple *contact* with external or shared reality has to be made, by "the infant's hallucinating and the world's presenting, with moments of illusion for the infant in which the two are taken by him to be identical, which they never in fact are."

> For this illusion to be produced in the baby's mind a human being has to be taking the trouble all the time to bring the world to the baby in understandable form, and in a limited way, suitable to the baby's need. For this reason a baby cannot exist alone, psychologically or physically, and really needs one person to care for him at first.
>
> The subject of illusion is a very wide one that needs study; it will be found to provide the clue to a child's interest in bubbles and clouds and rainbows, and all mysterious phenomena, and also to his interest in fluff, which is most difficult to explain in terms of instinct direct. Somewhere here, too, is the interest in breath, which never decides whether it comes primarily from within or without, and which provides a basis for the conception of spirit, soul, anima. (*CP*, p. 154)

Identity and perception are thus products of primary encounter, and out of these come our cultural powers.

To understand man's primary nature as *animal symbolicum,* we have to go back to the origins of his capacity to symbolize in play with the mother, as he begins to form his awareness of self and world. Observing the playing infant, says F. J. J. Buytendijk, the Dutch philosophical biologist:

> we already meet the ambiguous structure of genuine encounter, in a shadowy and elementary form, in the first erotic play of the moving, touching lips, tongue and hands of the nursing infant.[2]

To these aspects of meaningful physical encounter we may add all those complexities of fantasy to which Melanie Klein and D. W. Winnicott have drawn our attention. For instance, as well as the "ambiguity" of "grasping and being grasped," there are the ambiguities that arise in the child's mind between fantasy and reality (the fantasized feed and the actual feed). There are confusions between the "exciting" mother and the "rejecting" mother—an ambiguity reflected in his own movement between love (when "met" and satisfied) and hate (when the mother is not "there," or does not "meet" him but leaves him for a moment or rejects him).

In his studies of the meaning of play, Buytendijk sees that there is in human encounter something "surplus" over and above the "natural" foundation of animal life: "in the human case there is not only meeting of things, lures or threats, within the world, there is also something essentially different: loving encounter of person with person" (*AB*, p. 166).

I shall leave aside here for the moment the whole huge philosophical problem of how we "find" "the other": the implications of philosophical anthropology are that we *can*. Indeed, we are human and civilized because we have been able to develop in the context of encounter.

From the question of how in the life-sciences we may "know" a child, we may proceed to the question that is close to the humanities, how do we investigate a phenomenon between the functional and organic, and the cultural, such as *play?* This is evidently a topic around which totally new psychology and philosophy for student teachers could be developed in education, both in theory and in practice. The first clue Buytendijk uses to the meaning of play is to look at the meaning of the words in Dutch and Old Dutch. Play, he finds, connotes a *limited freedom of movement in limited space*. (In English *play* us used in this sense, of course, in engineering.) Then, using visual criteria, he detects a pattern that suggests to him that play can be understood as following necessarily from youthfulness.

This obviously relates to his theory of rank in living beings: higher animals have a period of youthfulness. In young creatures there is a readiness to change direction, and also a want of direction: *Ungerichtenheit*. The empirical scientist only finds passive babies' motions in response to "stimuli." Buytendijk finds "childish dynamics . . . a hybrid between expression and action"[3]—so he points to the intentional elements in it. There is a readiness to change direction, but a lack of overall directedness (neither is visible to the strict behaviorist), a diffuse mobility.

A second characteristic of youth is the drive to movement *(Bewegungsdrang)*. Here Marjorie Grene picks up the distinction Erwin Straus makes between *pathic* and *gnostic* modes of spatiality. The pathic mode is primitive and pervasive, the animal's original sensing of the qualities of his environment. The gnostic mode is directed to the *what* of the environment, and develops through the elaboration of perception into knowledge. Youthful behavior is characteristically pathic—"Youth does not yet live with the environment, is not yet directed to it." There is a nonfunctional, unorganized quality about it.

The pathic in the youthful organism, says Buytendijk, means ease of distraction, suggestibility, the tendency to follow and imitate the movement of living and nonliving bodies, and a naive relation to things. Straus has said that the inclination to dance is an expression of pathic spatiality. "Youth lives in a different space from adults." Finally, the naive state of relationship between young organism and environment is linked with shyness.

To Buytendijk play is a hedonic activity *(lustbetont)* but not coexistensive with pleasure-yielding activity as such. "Play is always playing with something," and in this sentence we may begin to follow the parallels between Buytendijk's phenomenology and that of D. W. Winnicott. "Something must also play with the player"; there is an intersubjective element in play.

> Both animals and men, Buytendijk says, play with images: with objects belonging to the in-between sphere of "fancy," the pathic half-light of the known and unknown. *(AB,* p. 153)[4]

All play needs a playground, and a certain rhythm of tension and relaxation. We cannot distinguish between play and earnest (children may play in earnest: love-play is serious). But playful trends, *when too much amplified,* tend to become serious reality. "Thus playing with a ball develops into sport; love-play into the sexual act; mock battle into battle" *(AB,* p. 153). Buytendijk noticed that girls play more than boys, who turn sooner to organized sport. In this he detects the pattern of a more pervasive "concern" *(Sorge).*

Buytendijk's interest in play, however, is in the element in it of *pathic communion,* which belongs to a vital level of existence underlying our intellectual and spiritual lives. It is this essential vitality that Dickens embodied in *Hard Times* in Sleary's horse-riding circus, and that Blake upheld against the Newtonian universe. Pathic communion, as in play, gives way to the life of the mind as a natural development of a "desire-free love," beyond the sphere of play. It is a different form of communion that we enter into here, one in which "the existence, and still more, the *value of the object* are sought and found" (emphasis added). This is very close to Winnicott's theory of the transitional object, the original cuddly rag or other play artifact, that is the bridge, after the stage of primitive body play, toward an adequate relationship with the other, and also the first symbol in the development of a personal culture.[5] In Buytendijk

> this new dimension depends for its being on our transcendence of the animal's rootedness in his specific environment. It begins with the child with his free-roving "curiosity" and moves on to the higher reaches of mental life. Such love, however, is an emergent from life, not its enemy. *(AB,* p. 154)

Characteristically human are both the growth of intellectual life in man (transcending the "how" of experience in favor of the "what" and the gnostic) *and* the persistence of playful activities in the adult.

Play entails a certain kind of spontaneous movement, and in this has its own symbolism. Play movements are often circular, capable of repetition and hence rhythmical:

> We see this in the rhythmic movement of infants, which are produced in circumstances of boredom, impatience or pain—wherever there is a situation of confinement, of "unfreedom." What is in question here, Buytendijk argues, is a spontaneous drive to movement in the youthful organism in the last analysis, a drive to freedom. (*AB,* p. 156)

"The action of the youthful organism," he argues, "is an *image* of the rational act of liberation."

> The drive to freedom is a constant, but the puppy or the baby, in its inexperience and want of objective direction, can express it only in a series of rhythmical or circular movements without a definite end in view. (Ibid.)

In the consequent rhythm of tension and relaxation, we get the essential dynamic of play. This hedonic movement, as in play, expresses most fully the significance of animal life in the "closed positionality." But in play there are also elements of *union.*[6] Thus there is a good deal in Buytendijk's theory of play that could be examined in the light of Winnicott's theories of union and separateness in "transitional object phenomena." Buytendijk also notes that "the child destroys an object because it offers resistance *and* because he wants to be united with it" (Grene, *AB,* p. 158).

Play here is not merely activity—the dance of gnats in the sun is not play. As we have already seen, "Play is always playing with something"— and so we have to look at the *plaything,* and this is, in fact, looking at a *symbol.*

Not all spontaneous movement is play. But even in spontaneous movement there may grow a meaning. Buytendijk sees in the actions of the youthful organism an *image of the act of liberation.* It will be clear, of course, from this that play is associated with the origin of culture and can be studied only phenomenologically—that is, by a subjective discipline, which can "find" such elements as freedom and "promise":

> Such movement has expressive value, as, for example, fidgeting. It also has a functional effect in turn on the organism itself, so that a functional cycle is established. In the consequent rhythm of tension and relaxation, the sense of "a promise that's kept," we get the essential dynamic of play.[7]

Objective psychology could never give an adequate account of the problems I have been discussing because it cannot find the way in which a "shaft of attention" goes out from the human being, who has been taught to perceive his world by his mother and by the processes of her responsiveness. It cannot find the being-in-the-world who is experiencing by a complex process of knowing rooted in body-life and tacit processes, emerging out of "being for" on the mother's part, much of it in play, and by imaginative processes. Marjorie Grene quotes Merleau-Ponty: "In order to perceive things we have to live them."

> In this active life with the world . . . things "show themselves, withdraw, approach, play games with us—and so are able to encounter us." (*Das Menschliche, Wege zu Seinem Verstandnis,* p. 71)

Merleau-Ponty uses here the difficult term *antepredicative,* which seems close to Polanyi's *tacit knowledge.* By this term he tries to indicate that our immediate perception of events takes place beyond—or before—the conceptual differentiation of the inert environment from being, toward which our whole existence is polarized. The thing offers itself to perceptive communication like a familiar face whose expression we completely understand. In such insights we can see that our capacity to perceive the world in a meaningful way is bound up with the way in which we gradually became capable of recognizing the mother's face (and her breast or body, together with her whole "handling"), and in this originates our capacity to experience the world in all those "antepredicative" ways that anticipate (in the proper sense of "go before") our relational-conceptual perception.

We have, that is, a feeling about the world, and things in it, and a feeling awareness of these, before we can say "I see . . ." or use the predicate, which expresses the "I" in relation to the "other" of the world. Those like Winnicott and Buytendijk who study the meaning of infant's play became aware of the complexities and subjectivities in knowing—the elements (we might say) S. T. Coleridge was aware of. Take, for instance, the elements of surrender and aggression discussed here, phenomenologically:

> The baby playing with his rattle displays a mixture of adaptive and aggressive dynamics, and his encounters with his toy prefigure our encounter with persons, in evoking tension and relaxation, expectation and surprise, grasping and being grasped, movement with and against, watching and showing oneself, listening and making oneself hear, surrender and liberation. (*Das Menschliche,* p. 75)

As we shall see, if we see the plaything as a transitional object—that is, a symbol of the experience of the mother, as "object" or "another" in symbolic form—this becomes even clearer.

Moreover, the infant play of making an object disappear, and then bringing it back, is seen as an experiment in testing existence itself, and a way of working, by a primitive form of poetry, on problems of being real, being in existence, and fearing one's annihilation by nothingness.[8]

As Marjorie Grene says, "It is impossible to tell exactly at first what moment the child first enters definitively into the human world." He looks at faces and responds—but so do animals. He looks back, but animals do too. "But with human encounter, in contrast, there is a surplus over and above the 'natural' foundation of animal life. In the human case there is not only meeting of things, lures, or threats, within the world: there is also something essentially different: *loving encounter of person with person*" (*AB*, p. 166).[9]

Play, as Susan Isaacs points out in *The Nursery Years*, begins at the mother's breast: as it becomes symbolic it involves a sense of three-term relationship between the self, the symbol, and the world. It is also the path toward give-and-take and the processes of love. Here is a sensitive account of a baby's symbolic "giving" in play by D. W. Winnicott. Here is the dawn of creativity in the individual:

> I place a spatula for him, and as he takes it his mother says: "He'll make more noise this time than last," and she is right. Mothers often tell me correctly what the baby will do, showing, if any should doubt it, that our picture gained in the out-patient department is not unrelated to life. Of course the spatula goes to the mouth and soon he uses it for banging the table or bowl. So to the bowl with many bangs. All the time he is looking at me, and I cannot fail to see that I am involved. In some way he is expressing his attitude to me. Other mothers and babies are sitting in the room behind the mother some yards away, and the mood of the whole room is determined by the baby's mood. A mother over the ways says: "He's the village black-smith." He is pleased with such success and adds to the play an element of showing off. He puts the spatula towards my mouth in a very sweet way, and is pleased that I play the game and pretend to eat it, not really getting in contact with it; he understands perfectly if only I show how I am playing his game. He offers it also to his mother, and then with a magnanimous gesture, turns round and gives it magically to the audience over the way. So he returns to the bowl and bangs go on.
>
> After a while he communicates in his own way with one of the babies on the other side of the room, choosing him from about eight grown-ups and children there. Everyone is now in a hilarious mood and the clinic is going very well.
>
> His mother now lets him down and he takes the spatula on the floor, playing with it and gradually edging over towards the other small person with whom he has just communicated by noises.
>
> You notice how he is interested not only in his own mouth, but also in mine and his mother's, and I think he feels he has fed all the people in the room. This he has done with the spatula, but he could not have done so if he had not just felt he had incorporated it, in the way I have described. (*CP*, p. 146)[10]

This most significant play—full of poetic symbolism—becomes more complex even before the baby can talk and walk.

Winnicott's importance is that he was a Freudian who completely reversed the Freudian pictures when it came to the place of culture. Freud,

Winnicott believed, never found a place for culture. Winnicott finds it in the intersubjectivity between mother and infant—in all those *imaginative processes* and forms of play by which the child comes to find himself, and his mother, and to experience the world as "out there" with its own reality. In short, play with the mother is the origin of the child's whole capacity to be a free adult in the world, and his culture is the instrument of that process, toward freedom and autonomy.

Winnicott's paper on this appears as a chapter in *Playing and Reality*. He says that "when one speaks of a man, one speaks of him along with the summation of his cultural experiences." Winnicott came to know this through his work with psychotic patients, who had not begun to be human. It was pointless to try to bring them through the usual experience of Freudian therapy, to release their instincts as far as was compatible with "society." They did not yet know what it was to be human, and they had no point to their lives. How was this point in life, and how was the sense of humanness to be achieved? Winnicott came to believe—*through culture*.

It is these cultural experiences that provide the continuity in the human race which transcends personal existence. (*LC*, p. 100)

Discussing the origins of identity, Winnicott refers to Middlemore's *The Nursing Couple* (1941) in which there is delineated "infinite richness in the intertwined techniques of the nursing couple" as a positive source of a feeling of being real and whole. By using its inner resources to build up a sense of the existence of its union with the mother (while she, of course, comes and goes in space and time), the baby comes to benefit from separation; here are the origins of autonomy and freedom:

This is the place that I have set out to examine. *The separation that is not a separation but a form of union.* (*PR*, p. 99)

This kind of experience differs in that it has no climax; it is not orgiastic, and does not bring that kind of satisfaction. It is thus not of the kind of psychosomatic functioning to which Freud devoted his attention, or that can be regarded, whether erroneously or not, as "instinctual." It belongs to intersubjectivity, even telepathy:

But these phenomena that have reality in the area whose existence I am postulating belong to *the experience of relating to objects*. One can think of the "electricity" that seems to generate in meaningful or intimate contact, and that is a feature when people are in love. (*PR*, p. 98)

In this way, obviously, psychoanalysis is recognizing that there are primary human "realities" that Freud could not find because he had concentrated on orgiastic experience.

> Psychoanalysts who have rightly emphasized the significance of instinctual experience and of reactions to frustration *have failed to state with comparable clearness or conviction the tremendous intensity of these non-climactic experiences that are called playing.* (*PR*, p. 98, emphasis added)

We have here Winnicott's thought emerging from his own Freudian background. Peter Lomas says that "certain elements in Winnicott's terminology remain unsatisfactory, for he has tried to retain Freudian 'metapsychology' in parts of his description," as by his use of the word *instinctual,* which can be challenged. Yet, as Lomas also says, "he conveys, even more vividly than Laing, the picture of *a self that remains its own agent*" (emphasis added). Psychoanalysis tends, says Winnicott, to think of ego-defenses and the anxiety that arises from the instinctual life: "we tend to think of health in terms of the state of ego-defences—we say it is more healthy when these defences are not rigid, etc." But

> You may cure your patient and not know *what it is that makes him or her go on living* . . . we have not yet started to describe what life is like apart from illness or the absence of illness. (*PR*, p. 58)

As Leslie H. Farber points out (in *The Ways of the Will*), there can be a tendency in psychoanalysis to conceive of a normative man in terms of the mere *absence* of illness, and with some kind of "health" perfectibility in the background. Winnicott's view is much more creative:

> That is to say, we have yet to tackle the question of *what life itself is about.* Our psychotic patients force us to give attention to this sort of basic problem . . . it is not instinctual satisfaction that makes a baby begin to be, to feel that life is real, to find life worth living. (*PR*, p. 98)

Obviously, what a baby takes in from its mother, in terms of "female element being" is something more than mere milk and comfort: it is a capacity to perceive the world, to love, and to develop symbols, and a sense of richness in the union—that which is meant by all the paintings in the world of Virgin and Child. By contrast, as Winnicott says, the Freudian restoration of instinctual functioning is mere "seduction" unless there is a personal meaning:

> Instinctual satisfactions start off as mere part-functions and they become *seductions* unless based on a well-established capacity in the individual person for total experience, and for experience in the area of transitional phenomena. *It is the self which must precede the self's use of instinct:* the rider must ride the horse, not be run away with . . . *"le style c'est l'homme même."* When one speaks of a man one speaks of him *along with* the summation of his cultural experience. The whole forms a unit. (*PR*, p. 99)

Here, indeed, we have a very different view of man from that of Freud's. From Winnicott's point of view, what must come first is human meaning, and the meaning of life, not "release." It is not the "id" that is most real about man, but his culture. In thinking about man in this way Winnicott is invoking culture, not as "sublimation" of instinctual drives, but as a *source of meaning in life,* a primary need. He is uncertain about whether he can define the word *culture,* but:

the accent indeed is on experience. In using the word culture I am thinking of the inherited tradition. I am thinking of something that is in the common pool of humanity, into which individuals and groups of people may contribute and from which we may all draw *if we have somewhere to put what we find.* (*PR,* p. 99)

This involves some kind of "recording method"—in which, obviously, Winnicott includes the language. This brings poetry, obviously, to a central place in personal development, in a way that was impossible to Freud. What also interests Winnicott is how

in any cultural field it is not possible to be original except on a basis of tradition . . . the interplay between originality and the acceptance of tradition as a basis for inventiveness seem to me to be just one more example, and a very exciting one, of the interplay between separateness and union. (*PR,* p. 99)

Thus, in the origins of our humanness in the interplay between union and separateness of the baby in his mother's care, we may find the origins of that interplay between union and separateness, between the individual and the culture, without which he cannot begin to be human. For too long has psychoanalysis implied that to be truly human is to merely *function* as an organism.

It is of first importance for us to acknowledge openly that absence of psychoneurotic illness may be health but it is not life. Psychotic patients who are hovering all the time between living and not living force us to look at this problem, one which really belongs not to psychoneurotics but to all human beings. I am claiming that these same phenomena that are life or death to our schizoid or borderline patients appear in our cultural experiences. It is these cultural experiences that provide the continuity in the human race which transcends personal existence. I am assuming that cultural experiences are in direct continuity with play, the play of those who have not yet heard of games. (*PR,* p. 100)

Culture then arises out of "the potential space between the subjective object and the object objectively perceived, between me-extensions and the not-me," and cultural development is thus at one with the discovery of actuality—"there being objects and phenomena outside omnipotent control." It is thus hand in hand with what Winnicott calls "disillusion"—the gradual sense of omnipotence, magical powers, and monism, which are necessary to the baby at the beginning, but which could only impede his capacities to live if they were not relinquished as he grows.

In cultural growth an important concept for Winnicott is "trust": culture grows out of the primal relationship in which the mother is "being for" the child.

The basis of the individual's sense of meaning in life is thus bound up with his capacity to trust, in regard to which Winnicott quotes a Jungian analyst, A. Plaut:

> The capacity to form images and to use these constructively by recombinations into new patterns is—unlike dreams of fantasies—dependent on the individual's ability to trust.[11]

The "formative principle" in each individual is thus drawn out by trust, and it links the individual with his whole culture, because the symbols he draws on increasingly to develop his sense of meaning and identity are taken from every source in his civilization:

> it is these cultural experiences that provide the continuity in the human race which transcends personal existence.

But culture always maintains the two elements that are given it by its origins. The "transitional object" or first symbol has two aspects. It stands for the inward possession of the mother, and so enables the individual to grow toward separateness and independence, carrying his "lifebelt," which symbolizes adequate psychic parturition. At the same time, since it symbolizes union with the mother, it enables the individual to take advantage of further and further ranges of union, to take more and more into himself by his creative possession of artifacts. As the transitional object is "decathected" and ceases to be the focus of emotional attention, other cultural interests take its place.

In his theory of culture Winnicott sees the infant as making use of an object in a very special way, one in which the adult plays a special role:

> An essential part of any formulation of transitional phenomena is that . . . we agree never to make the challenge to the baby: did you create this object or did I? . . . *for the baby* (if the mother can supply the right conditions) every detail of the baby's life is an example of creative living. Every object is a "found" object. Given the chance, the baby begins to live creatively, and to use actual objects to be creative into. If the baby is not given this chance then there is no area in which the baby may have play, or may have cultural experience; then there is no link with the cultural inheritance, and there will be no contribution to the cultural pool.

The "depri ved child" is notoriously restless and unable to play, and has an impoverishment of capacity to experience in the cultural field. (P. 271)

The "potential space" in which culture exists only happens *in relation to a feeling of confidence* on the part of the baby, that is, confidence related to the dependability of the mother-figure or environmental elements.

From Winnicott's point of view a disturbed child is destructive or delinquent because he is trying to claim by his aggression the love that is due to him. This may involve the child in ferocious attacks on "transitional objects" that should be symbols but do not yield sufficient "play" satisfaction because they have not become part of "creative living," and there is no link through them with "the cultural inheritance." To understand such delinquency we have to try to understand its symbolism.

I have discussed the work of D. W. Winnicott in conjunction with that of F. J. J. Buytendijk, and it is possible to link the work of these with that of Helmuth Plessner and the philosophy of Martin Buber. What unites all these approaches is their phenomenological quality, and their existentialist sense that in trying to understand human experience one must recognize that one is dealing with living beings. Buytendijk was a physiologist and a comparative psychologist, and his concern was to forge adequate conceptual tools for the study of behavior. He believed that in trying to understand human beings, we need to participate in an existential way in encountering them. (I have already related this perspective and Marjorie Grene's analysis of it, to education, in *English for Meaning* [Reading, Eng.: National Foundation for Educational Research, 1980], p. 109.)

"Without the foundation in our own being, our own existential participation in encountering others, we should have no access to the phenomenon we have set out to investigate." Buytendijk's methodology involves us in keeping in mind that "each person chooses his way of being in the world"; we need to keep in mind the unique individual dynamic of each person, his identity and his capacity to perceive the world as real and meaningful; "he makes his world the world it is, by his projection of it."

We go out to meet a world that equally comes to meet us:

"In the concreteness of existence, every objective perception, in its indissoluble union with intentional movement, is produced only out of a *productive encounter* of man with his environment." (V. F. von-Weizsäcker, *Der Gestaltkreis* [Leipzig: G. Thieme, 1943] quoted in *AB*, p. 164)

Buytendijk observes that we have to take the "risk of knowing *Dasein,* if we are to study such a phenomenon as encounter." But, says Marjorie Grene, there is another risk, which is

> to acknowledge the being of the individual existent as questioner *and* of the real relation of two individuals in mutual question and response. (*AB*, p. 167)

In order to understand man we have to take the risk of experiencing and confronting love and the ultimate problems of meaning.

If we place together the observation of the philosophical biologists, and the insights of the psychoanalysts who have worked with children, we can see how they illuminate the value of creative effort as a way of finding oneself in relation to others. As Buber said, "Man becomes conscious of his transcendence in the I-Thou relationship, in which he is assured of his freedom."

> An object like a tree or an animal can speak to man as a Thou, but the I-Thou relationship is mostly between man and man. The I-Thou relationship requires two whole people to conduct the genuine dialogue in which "each should regard his partner as the very one he is," accepting him and confirming him as a partner. (*EN*, p. 43)

Buber, like Jaspers, complained that the present age is not conducive to the development of I-Thou relationships. But every human being who can speak, be autonomous, and walk about demonstrating his existential freedom has achieved these powers through the I-Thou relationship with the mother, in which play is a primary and major element. The study of how these capacities develop is surely crucial to the humanities and education.

Moreover, as we have seen, integral with the development of play is the question of conscience—that is, the moral issue—because the symbolism of play is devoted to the discovery of concern. That is, one "finds" the other in play, and at the same time finds the sense of meaning in life by developing concern for the other. As Ledermann says,

> Conscience can be unconscious, but it can be elevated[12] into consciousness or can be suppressed. The man who hears the call of conscience, who is conscious of his tasks in life, finds life meaningful and becomes aware of the road to authenticity. (*EN*, p. 46)

The development of a "personalistic existential ethic" or a sense of meaning or authenticity in oneself, begins in play—and so to foster opportunities for play, and for the cultural activity to which it leads, is the clue to the promotion of human freedom in the existentialist sense.

I believe that it is an intuitive grasp of this that has led so many students, in my experience, to turn to work with children, as by teaching in infants' schools or in working with children in need of care. They have found there, in the midst of a dehumanized world, a clue to the pursuit of meaning and humanness.

Here, then, are indicators to a form of study, gladly embracing the insights of philosophical anthropology, which, far from striving to be detached and "objective" becomes both a process of growth in the student and a means to promote humanness itself. In this chapter I have tried to offer a glimpse of what the new disciplines in philosophical anthropology may yield as we learn to accept and develop them.

Notes

1. Winnicott puts this in, and I leave it in, to avoid causing anxiety by a literal interpretation. "The breast" can mean the bottle—and, indeed, means the whole experience of the mother, in all ways.

2. F. J. J. Buytendijk, *Das Menschliche, Wege zu seines Verständnis* trans. Marjorie Grene in *AB* (Stuttgart, 1958), p. 72.

3. *Das Spiel bei Mensch und Tier* (Berlin: Wolff, 1933).

4. I discuss Buytendijk's theory as Marjorie Grene expands it because the essays in question are not accessible in English elsewhere.

5. See "The Location of Culture," in *Playing and Reality*.

6. Buytendijk here illuminates much that is the subject of a strange poem by Sylvia Plath, *The Night Dances*. See my discussion in *Sylvia Plath: Poetry and Existence*.

7. Buytendijk, discussed by Marjorie Grene (*AB*, p. 156). How the quest for "freedom" of the autonomous creature is expressed in play, and its meanings, may also be studied in Marjorie Grene. For a further account of Buytendijk's relation to phenomenology see "Husserl's Phenomenology" by D. O'Connor and N. Lawrence, *Readings in Existential Phenomenology* (Englewood Cliffs, N.J.: Prentice Hall, 1967).

8. See Len Chaloner, *Feeling and Perception in Young Children,* which is a phenomenological study, though Chaloner would not have known that it was. The Susan Isaacs tradition is itself phenomenological.

9. See Kurt Goldstein, "The Smiling of the Infant and the Problem of Understanding the Other," *Journal of Psychology* 54 (1957): 175–91, in which Plessner and Buytendijk are both invoked.

10. The chapters *"Appetite and Emotional Disorder"* (1936) and *"The Observation of Infants in a Set Situation"* (1941) in D. W. Winnicott's *Collected Papers* are full of phenomenological observations of this kind.

11. A. Plaut, "Reflections about not Being Able to Imagine," *Journal of Analytical Psychology* 2 (1966).

12. Ledermann refers us here to Martin Buber, "Guilt and Guilt Feelings," in *Knowledge of Man,* ed. M. Friedmann, (London: George Allen and Unwin, 1965), pp. 126–27.

6

Learning as an Activity of the Whole Being: Implications of the Work of Michael Polanyi

Perhaps the major insight from philosophical anthropology for the humanities is its radical approach to the nature of learning. Sensing and perceiving are seen as dynamics in a living process involving the whole being. Even to see what learning is and what knowledge is requires a new way of examining the modes of existence of complex beings in their life world.

The rediscovery of Husserl in our time, as phenomenology comes into its own, is at one with a rediscovery of his insistence of learning as growth:

> Learning is not the *accumulation* of scraps of knowledge. It is a *growth*, where every act of knowledge develops the learner, thus making him capable of constituting ever more and more complex objectivities—and the objective growth in complexity parallels the subjective growth in capacity. (Husserl, as interpreted by Quentin Lauer, *The Triumph of Subjectivity*, p. 29)

To understand how we may make headway here, we must study further the work of Michael Polanyi, especially in his *Personal Knowledge*. He showed that the established "facts" of science, however unquestioned, are still held in being by the same intellectual passions that first discovered them: they are conjectures.[1] They may be so amply and confidently attested that no one "in his senses"—that is no one who accepts the authority of competent scientific opinion—would call them in doubts; but science, the late James Franck suggested, "is either something scientists are doing, or it is nothing at all," while "nothing any human being does has the wholly assured, wholly self-evident character of Cartesian method." The truth of this statement is impressively demonstrated in the argument of *Personal Knowledge,* declares Marjorie Grene.

I have used Marjorie Grene so far in this book as a stimulus, in opening up questions of the nature of knowing in an anti-Cartesian way. Her work in philosophy very largely derives from Polanyi's exploration, as a scientist, of the nature of knowing, and his conclusions are of tremendous importance in this whole debate.

Polanyi's opening section is headed "The Art of Knowing." In it he emphasizes that knowing is a mysterious act performed by whole persons, employing powers that cannot be made fully articulate, that cannot be fully analyzed, and that are not accessible or available to control; they are ineffable.

There is no knowledge except by the *personal participation* of the knower in all acts of understanding. Articulate knowledge is in the end something of which we have "focal awareness," but we arrive at it by the exercise of skills, and in this we operate by "subordinating a sort of particulars" as clues or tools, of which we are "subsidiarily aware." "These clues or tools are made to function as extensions of our bodily equipment and this involves a certain change of our own being." But we cannot be explicitly aware of the processes, cannot follow them or command them at all points, or reduce them to analytic logic or schematization (thus no computer or electronic model can ever serve as a model of human intelligence).

The participation of the knower has important implications for questions of value and meaning: it enables us to overcome the alienations and dissociations of "objectivity." Personal knowledge is an intellectual commitment and as such is "inherently hazardous"—it is a mode of being-in-the-world. But Polanyi's insights also have important implications for knowledge itself, about how it is known, and what it is, as we shall see.

Polanyi, as we have seen, demolishes early the false goal of "objectivity." All our knowledge, all our inquiry into truth, has a *human perspective,* unless we are to be absurd.

When one system replaces another, as when the Copernican System replaced the Ptolemaic, this was because the new system offers a satisfaction that is really subjective—it "preferred to satisfy a different human satisfaction." Of course, the new theory was also more objective, in that it had an inherent quality deserving universal acceptance by rational creatures: it commends respect in its own right by its very rationality, so it is more than a mere personal, subjective choice.

But what good new scientific theories produce is "intellectual satisfaction" and this is not "objective." Moreover, a good theory has an intentional and even idealistic component: it inspires us "with the hope of overcoming the appalling disabilities of our bodily existence," with a Pygmalion impulse. Science is thus rooted in passion and faith. In *Personal Knowledge* Polanyi examines the general assumption of "objectivity." Suppose we made an enormous film of the history of the universe over the last 4,000,000,000 years. Man's whole era would occupy only one frame. His existence would pass in a flash. Is that how—"objectively"—

we want to see the reality of existence? In fact, of course, we are interested in the whole only because of that flash-moment of human existence and the relation of everything to it.

Even our most rigorous explorations are thus anthropocentric, and also subjective in that, like Copernicus's model of the universe that replaced the Ptolemaic, they satisfy us more. Each step forward in science has its aesthetic component, and scientists are deeply committed to their work, often with passion. For instance, I recently heard a young American astonomer say on the radio that he would "like to live his life all over again" because certain new techniques in telescope work promise to reveal such extraordinary new facts about distant galaxies.

The nihilistic view that only "matter" is "real" has a long history, of course. Democritus said, "By convention coloured, by convention sweet, by convention bitter: in reality only atoms and the void." But the kind of skepticism I have referred to above may be traced to the positivistic philosophy that arose in the nineteenth century. It denied to the scientific theories of physics any claim to coherent rationality, a claim that it condemned as metaphysical and mystical. Scientific theory must not go beyond experience by affirming anything that cannot be tested by experience. According to the strict principles of positivism, theory must be dropped as soon as an observation comes along that conflicts with it (see Ernst Mach, *Die Mechanik*, 1883). But as Polanyi shows, not even those who believe this behave like it.

Polanyi declares that the kind of philosophy to which positivism and "objective" science cling is absurd, but it is the inevitable consequence of separating, in principle, mathematical knowledge from empirical knowledge. Mach was absurd because he wanted to exorcise that very capacity of the human mind by which new theories of certain kinds emerge—the example Polanyi takes being Einstein's theory of relativity, which was a product of that very rationality which positivism wishes to eliminate from the foundation of science.

Polanyi goes on to celebrate the passionate participation of the scientist in the act of knowing. The act of knowing includes an appraisal, and this "personal coefficient" shapes all factual knowledge. Because all science involves personal judgment, aesthetic aspects, intuitions, and creativity, we can never separate the knower from the known, while the involvement of the knower in knowledge redeems that universe from its apparent alienation.[2] From Polanyi's recognition of the personal nature of knowledge, we may build bridges between subjectivity and objectivity. In this discussion poetry and science may meet: it is not a question of "two cultures" but of the reintegration of sensibility. The question resolves itself into one of *modes of thinking* and their difference: both the artist and the scientist are trying to make sense of the world.

There are always tacit assumptions in knowledge. Polanyi uses the analogy of some stones arranged on the garden of a railway station, to read WELCOME TO WALES. Could they have arranged themselves by chance? Mathematical calculation can crush any such argument. Suppose the station master dies, and the stones become scattered. Now we are not prepared to say they did *not* come like that by chance. These examples show that there was an assumption from the beginning that these stones arranged themselves in a distinctive pattern, in an orderliness. It was only in view of this orderliness that we asked the question about orderliness. So, in many exploration of the nature of things, especially living things, we make assumptions of this kind about orderliness; we are interested in the things only because of this element. There is an implicit assumption that we take for granted—but then ignore! In many approaches to the nature of living organisms we are interested because of a *distinctive pattern of living.* Can such orderliness have come into existence by random coincidence? We are often asked to believe this, even though it can be shown that it was extremely improbable. The explanation of the existence of certain living things, which display a significant order, requires the existence of an *ordering principle.*

What can this possibly mean? Yet the denial of any such thing, it seems to Polanyi, is sustained only by a logical muddle. The truth is that we recognize that a human being is more substantial than a pebble, because the human being has a self-awareness and a consciousness: and, as E. W. F. Tomlin declares, it is unbelievable that consciousness could have come by accident. The orderliness and form in life, and its essential directiveness cannot, certainly, be denied: and these flower in mind.

Polanyi goes on to suggest that we, that "human events," that personal achievement, and that subjectivity, are, in fact, *more real* than pebbles and stars. Our *knowing* is more real than "matter in motion." There is something else in the universe than matter, as Marjorie Grene says; there is knowing mind. This reversal, evidently, is of enormous importance to us in the arts and education. It should encourage us to challenge that prevalent materialistic view of the universe which makes us feel our achievements in the realm of symbolism are mere sand castles, to be swept away by the next tide of matter. "Responsibility" is a key word in this philosophical discussion. Polanyi rescues us from the situation of being helpless inhabitants of a bleak and remorseless, alien universe, but depicts us as being the sole bearers of the mystery of *knowing* that universe—a position that imposes upon us immense responsibilities, not least to our own evolution.

Polanyi speaks of the "beauty and power" inherent in the rationality of contemporary physics, and points out, discussing theories of relativity, that this positivist separation is unreal. All scientific discovery requires *appraisal,* and a passionate participation. Scientists certainly do not drop a theory as soon as anything comes along that conflicts with it. There is a personal involvement, and personal knowledge is manifested in the appreciation of probability and order in the exact sciences, while the descriptive sciences (like biology) rely on skills and connoisseurship. The supposed "objectivity" of positivism, like Descartes' clear and distinct ideas, is a delusion and a false ideal.

The aim of the exact sciences is to establish complete control over experience in terms of precise rules that can be formally set out and empirically tested. By discussing questions of probability Polanyi shows that this is impossible; personal judgment always has to be exercised. In dealing with the world we can never merely follow the rules; having ascribed all truth and error to an exact theory of the universe, we always have to exercise personal judgment even the strictest scientific analysis.

If we accept this element of appraisal, then we are in a position to reexamine certain radical assumptions in modern science. In its positivist paradigm it doggedly denies any recognition of order in the universe. All cosmic events are governed by chance, and have occurred accidentally. This implies a denial that they are governed by order. Thus, when it comes to the theories of evolution, that living species have come into being by accidental mutations, we find that science credits the distinctive patterns of living beings as exhibiting a peculiar orderliness which is why we are interested in them. It is that this science trusts itself to appraise: yet at the same time science is obliged to believe that evolution has taken place by a vastly improbable coincidence of random events combining into an orderly shape of a highly distinctive character. This is a logical muddle, and Polanyi's purpose in opening the question up is to reveal the assumptions, in terms of personal appraisal, that underlie the so-called objective procedures of science. In the logical muddle examined above, we find a piece of equivocation "unconsciously prompted by the urge to avoid facing the problem set to us by the fact that the universe has given birth to these curious beings, including people like ourselves" (*PK*, p. 35). That is, in such scientific thought we find an implicit metaphysic, which involves the denial, or evasion, of the metaphysical problem. This, of course, has a devastating effect on the humanities.

Such examinations of the logical confusions in the idea science holds of itself reveals the whole life-world of individuals, some of whom make up "the world of science." Serious errors arise when, by its extrapolation into a metaphysic, science assumes the right to tell us what the world is like—what the world *is* and what life is, within it. The traditional categories in epistemology are "objective" and "subjective," but Polanyi points to a substantial alternative—giving credit to our capacity to make "valid appraisals of universal bearings within the exact sciences." This opens up the question, that even the exact and so-called objective sciences are disciplines within a much wider and more complex operation of skills.

Applying this to education, we could say that there could never be a fully explicit analytical account of the processes of teaching and learning and it is a largely absurd and fruitless undertaking to seek to construct theories and rules for a teacher to follow, to do his job. He can only employ his skills as an art and how these are used and what they are can never be fully and explicitly known, for they too are ineffable. It is as a *scientist* that Polanyi knew that even in using the sets of formulae that the exact sciences employ as "bearing on experience" we rely upon our powers of *personal knowing* in accrediting this bearing. Science is operated by the skill of the scientist, and it is through the exercise of his skill that he shapes his scientific knowledge.

Polanyi next goes on to the "well-known fact" that the aim of a skillful performance is achieved by the observance of a set of rules "which are not known as such by the person following them." Obvious examples are swimming and bicycling: who can really say what they do, to stay afloat as a swimmer or upright on a bicycle? Swimmers do not know that they breathe differently to stay afloat in the water; cyclists do not know that they turn to the left as they begin to fall to the left. To know the rules, and to attempt to apply them explicitly, will simply lead, as with the beginner, to falling off. The real knowledge of how to ride a bicycle is inexplicit, and belongs to body-life, and to experience. It is a *skill:* the rider "dwells in" his bicycle.

One consequence of the scientific revolution has been a difficulty in accepting the reality of skills. Of course, in some areas the demand for "scientific proof" has helped to substitute realities for superstitions. But there are industries in which skills and arts were producing goods, but in which science has to make enormous efforts even to find out what is going on (e.g., brewing, textiles, and potteries). Arts in such areas can be passed on by apprenticeship, by experience, but cannot be passed on by explicit "scientific" instruction, and skills can be irretrievably lost. As Polanyi points out, no scientific effort could reproduce a Stradivarius violin.

Much of the learning in apprenticeship is *unconscious,* and some of the rules and practices that are learned are not explicitly known, even to the master! These skills are passed on by imitation, and so any society that wants to preserve this kind of personal knowledge must submit to tradition.

In this recognition of the "tacit" elements in skills and learning, we have much that is relevant to education. There is a lack of skills and satisfactions in our society that may well be due to the assumption, predominant in our educational system, that explicit instruction and the learning of theories and rules, as in mathematics and the physical sciences, is the way both to learn skills and to develop competence. In countering this lies the value of genuine creative work, for in painting, music, creative writing, dance, and other expressive arts we learn and develop skills in quite different, nonexplicit (female) ways. We have to cooperate with our daimon. And in working life, as Polanyi argues, the doctor in diagnosis, the wine-taster, the tea-blender, and such professionals can acquire skills only by "the art of knowing." And, in the end, we have to admit that the same is really true of the scientist, too, for "the art of knowing has remained unspecifiable at the very heart of science" (*PK*, p. 55).

Going on to discuss specific skills, Polanyi treats of our experience in such a simple skill as driving in a nail with a hammer, when we have a *subsidiary awareness* of the feeling in the palm of our hand, which is merged into the *focal awareness* of driving in the nail. Our subsidiary awareness of such a tool makes it a part of our own body, and we dwell in it, as part of the whole meaning of driving in the nail:

> We pour ourselves into them and assimilate them as parts of our own existence. We accept them existentially by dwelling in them. (*PK*, p. 59)

The same is true of other mental tools—language, mathematical concepts, mental signs, symbols—we dwell in them, and are existentially extended into them.

> This reliance is a personal commitment which is involved in all acts of intelligence by which we integrate some things subsidiarily to the centre of our focal attention. Every act of personal assimilation by which we make a thing from an extension of ourselves through our subsidiary awareness of it, is a commitment of ourselves; a manner of disposing of ourselves. (*PK*, p. 61)

It is clear from this that learning and knowledge can never be separated from persons knowing. Yet how we integrate the clues in these processes (as by interpreting the operations of a probe, like a blind man using a stick in the dark) we do not and cannot know. By unconscious trial and error we feel our way to success. If we concentrate on the particulars we fall off the bicycle or become unable to play the piano. (This kind of thing we often experience. When someone comes in the room perhaps we are playing better than we thought we could; but their presence tends to convey the inquiry, "how did you come to play that so well?" and at once we become aware of our fingers and can play no more.)

By becoming imbued with subsidiary awareness, the particulars that we have made extensions of our body may form a coherent focal entity; and this indicates standards—an obligation toward the truth, an effort to submit to reality.

Knowing and learning are therefore much more complex than we thought and involve whole beings and their growth. Moreover, any act of learning "commits us, passionately and far beyond our comprehension, to a vision of reality." As Ursula's experience in *The Rainbow,* discussed above, indicates, too much in education fails to recognize this, and remains a passionless rigmarole that does not really advance learning at all. Of how much in education dare we say, with scientist Polanyi:

> Like love, to which it is akin, this commitment is a "shirt of flame", blazing with passion and, also like love, consumed by devotion to a universal demand. (*PK,* p. 64)

Such is even the devotion to objective science! All knowing is seen by Polanyi's account to involve "*an intentional change of being*"—the "pouring of ourselves into the subsidiary awareness of particulars" toward a comprehensive whole, in which act standards are inevitably involved—and in which we are concerned in the end with existential meaning.

I want now to go on Polanyi's penultimate chapter in *Personal Knowledge,* chapter 12, entitled "*Knowing Life.*" Polanyi has tried to show that our knowing is ultimately ineffable: we do not and cannot know how we know. The tacit processes, such as subception, indwelling, and the integration of clues, though they may lead to explicit knowledge, to "focal awareness," can never be subjected to comprehensive analysis, and cannot be reduced to logical steps; for this reason alone any kind of mechanical or computer model of the human mind must be false. The goal of modeling thinking by a machine is fallacious and can never be achieved.

While these things are true of the knower, they have radical implications for the known. The recognition of personal knowledge actually redeems the universe, because it leads to that conclusion already referred to, that "there *is* something else in the universe other than matter in motion—there is knowing mind." Especially redeemed is the category of life, because it is clear that *knowing life* requires a quite different mode of understanding from that of the physical sciences—and many serious errors come from the failure of scientists, even those studying life, to recognize this simple truth.

Facts about living things, says Polanyi, are more highly personal than the facts of the inanimate world. We have to exercise even more personal faculties in order to understand life:

> For when an organism operates more as a machine or more by a process of equipotential integration, our knowledge of its achievements must rely on a comprehensive appreciation of it which cannot be specified in terms of mere impersonal facts. (*PK,* p. 347)

As we study the higher animals our understanding of them requires more and more, in us, of the exercise of the very faculties we are trying to study in them, and because these are not accessible to full explicit or logical analysis we have to devise other ways of understanding. *"Biology is life reflecting on itself."*

The word *achievements* in the above quotation, should be noted, by the way, for it is impossible to discuss life without some such term and concept. As Polanyi points out, while both thunderstorms and elephants are self-sustaining systems, it would be ridiculous to talk of the "achievement" of a thunderstorm; but of an elephant it can be seen as an achievement of life in evolution, and we can speak of achievement in connection with the elephant. To invoke another insight from Polanyi, "life strives."[3]

The biologist's commitment involves the accrediting of the realities of which living requires a recognition of more than the physical components of life. As found by microreductionism, it pursues a line that moves from the I-It to the I-Thou, to borrow those useful terms from Buber. Not only are the objects of attention in biology *subjects* and *beings,* but understanding them belongs to a relationship that invokes intelligence, involving the knowing that culminates in human greatness.

Polanyi then discusses the practice of classification, which is important in the life sciences. Classical taxonomy is not in the present climate a highly valued scientific activity. Our present kind of valuation of knowledge seems to involve a distaste for certain forms of knowing and being, "a growing reluctance to credit ourselves with the capacity for personal knowing, and a corresponding unwillingness to recognize the reality of the unspecifiable entities established by such knowing" (*PK,* p. 350).

Taxonomy requires what C. F. S. Pantin called "aesthetic recognition." Polanyi compares the work of the biologist with that of the crystallographer: the biologist's standards are empirical; they are

> shaped piece-meal by a series of conceptional decisions, made by a close observation of every new specimen to be subsumed under the species to which it is thought to belong. Thus every time a specimen is appraised, the standards of normality are somewhat modified so as to make them approximate more closely to what is truly normal for the species. These standards are themselves subject to appraisal by the biologist. (*PK,* p. 349)

This element of appraisal, as a kind of participation, has implications for the nature of knowledge that the strict positivist dislikes; while it also indicates the ineffable quality of what is known in biology. Each "specimen" is a being, which is recognized at one and the same time as a unique individual and as belonging to a species. Inevitably, there are subjective elements both in the knowing and in the known—and so we are brought to the recognition that the study of living beings derives its value from the *intrinsic* interest of living things. This restores to our view of science the recognition of the intellectual passions involved and the contemplative value in science.

These elements need to be recognized in some of the more dynamic and complex areas of biology. For example, one area Polanyi goes on to discuss is that of the growth of organisms. He discusses both remedial growth (some organisms being able to grow a whole new creature from a tiny piece of themselves) and embryonic growth. There are in such areas both processes that move straightforwardly by the rational concurrence of several parts with fixed functions *and* achievements performed by the equipotential interplay of all parts of a system. In studying living organisms the scientist takes their systems apart with a view to discovering how each part functions in conjunction with the other parts, and this may penetrate with the physical and chemical mechanisms. But the overall investigation begins from some anterior knowledge of the system's total performance and the meaning of the work will always lie on its bearing on living structures that are true to type, emerging from a mosaic of morphogenetic fields.

The appreciation of true shapes and of significant structures involves personal knowledge, and this disturbs scientists because it seems to be half-way toward an unreconcilable paradigm. In a sense scientists (like molecular biologists) seem to be reducing everything to physics. Yet their work inevitably *takes notice of* living beings and tacitly recognizes that an elephant *is* different from a thunderstorm. The basis of the recognition of these special features of living beings lies in a totally different kind of scientific philosophy. The "Laplacean" kind of knowledge cannot find "life," since no complete topographical chart of the physicochemical changes involved in any life process could account for it in a significant way. It could, after a superhuman effort, only convey to us what our ordinary insight conveys about morphogenesis.

We recognize and understand the processes of life by the observation and understanding of patterns and processes, just as we try to observe and understand the behavior of the higher animals. Such approaches to the concept of life are inescapably personal, and it would seem that what Polanyi is demanding are new modes of thought in this dimension. At the moment, however, the drive of the life-sciences is rather toward micro-reduction, and the belief that breaking the processes down, and mathematical analysis, will produce the explanations we need. The use of computers to solve fantastic mathematical problems adds conviction to this belief; so Sidney Brenner is quoted as believing that with tissue cultures linked to computers we could grow a hand.[5] This is to turn an accepted mode of knowing life back into a life-creating process. The implication of Polanyi's philosophy would seem to be that knowing life depends on whole capacities of human understanding that cannot be reduced to mathematics or straightforward logic of that kind, nor can the qualities and systems in life that are being studied be so reduced. To suppose that a mathematicizing logical computer could grow a hand is therefore absurd, since living tissue does not function in that way and is not governed by that kind of simplification; it is not simple like that and *cannot be*. New modes of apprehension may even be said to be necesssary to understand the "category of life," and these will not be like those which excel in physics and mathematics. They will rather belong to those modes by which (tacitly) even the strictest molecular biologist chooses his living subjects and apprehends their difference from other physical entities. They involve the structures and processes that are thus tacitly recognized, as when the morphogenetic powers of an individual creature do not operate in a linear way, and do not even operate under the government of a single organizer, but under subcenters of organization, increasingly divided into secondary and even tertiary organizers but always serving the dynamics of the whole organism.[6] In this debate we are not moving toward "vitalism" but rather suggesting different dimensions in life, with overall complex hierarchical principles that are tacitly recognized in "life-science" but implicitly denied by the assumptions of work based solely on physics and mathematics.

Organs and their functions exist only in their bearing on the presumed interest of the living individual, so all physiology is teleological, and in such work we may speak of reasons and causes. The existence of a living being is, in the flux of life, an aim in itself, and so, behind our investigations, stands a conception of "how it ought to be."

In this area of biology there is a clash between the tacit recognition of the *achievement* in living things and the mechanistic dogma that all living machinery has come into existence by accident and is found in existence only because evolution has conferred on individual being competitive advantages that have secured their survival. There are those (like Pierre-Paul Grassé) who challenge this dogma, saying that it is impossible to reconcile it with the facts. It would eliminate any true achievement from the phylogenesis of living things. But even so it would make no difference to the inherent meaning of the recognition of jointly functioning organs, which is a teleological one—the implied goal in such processes of life.

In these chapters, as elsewhere, the value of Polanyi's writing is to bring back to our attention certain aspects of existence and especially certain aspects of our thought that we have forgotten, or have come to pretend do not exist; and with these, of course, certain realities in the world. The aim of his book, says Polanyi, is to "re-equip men with the faculties which centuries of critical thought have taught them to distrust" (*PK*, p. 381).

To counteract the "crippling mutilations imposed by an objectivist framework," we have a new task, that of "reinterpreting the world as it is."

Polanyi makes an absolute distinction between the living and the nonliving, in the sense that the living needs to have applied to it the distinction of success or failure. Systems that can succeed or fail are properly characterized by operational principles or what he calls "rules of rightness." One cannot define things that are characterized by a rule of rightness in terms that are neutral to that rightness. Polanyi believes that there must be an *ordering principle* that *originated life* and that promotes evolutionary development: an *"orderly innovating principle."* Rather than see the inanimate matter that is the context of life as the only source of life, Polanyi wishes to interpret it as the *condition* that *sustains* life, "and the accidental configuration of matter from which life had started . . . merely *released* the operations of life" (*PK*, p. 384).

The action of an ordering principle cannot be found by conventional theories of natural selection, because it cannot be accounted for in terms of accidental mutation plus natural selection. Mutation and selection, Polanyi believes, should be seen in the light of the recognition of an ordering principle as ways of merely *releasing and sustaining the action of evolutionary principles* by which all major evolutionary achievements are defined.

The *consecutive* steps of a long-range evolutionary progress—like the rise of human consciousness—cannot be determined merely *by their adaptive advantage,* since these advantages can form part of such progress only *insofar as they prove adaptive in a peculiar way, namely, on the lines of a continuous, ascending, evolutionary achievement.* And this can only be appraised by us. Polanyi believes that established evolutionary theory has failed to take in this element of appraisal, which, when applied, makes certain evident facts plain.

> . . . we need no abstract analysis to recognise than an orderly transforming principle has been at work. We have direct evidence, anticipating the result of our logical analysis, in the manifest rise of human consciousness. From a seed of submicroscopic living particles—and from inanimate beginnings lying beyond these—we see emerging a race of sentient, responsible and creative beings. The spontaneous rise of such incomparably higher forms of being testifies to the operations of an orderly innovating principle. (*PK*, pp. 386–87)

Science is a high product of evolution, and is an achievement of human culture and consciousness. We follow science and we are interested in the universe, matter, and man, because of man's existence. Man is the first reality with which we have to deal, and the ordering principle that produced man is our beginning. Human consciousness could never have been created by chance—that is surely the first reality to be recognized. It could only be the product of that principle which seeks, in the context of matter, feeding on matter, operating within the dynamics of matter, to fulfill itself, to *achieve* potentialities.

From that recognition we go back, to see how the higher human powers emerged from the powers of the higher animals (Polanyi makes some useful parallels between human child and ape offspring) and how these emerged from lower forms, from primitive forms, and from inanimate matter (for there is no break between animate and inanimate; see A. Frey-Wissling, *Submicroscopic Morphology of Protoplasm* [New York: Elsevier, 1953]).

From this kind of perspective (and Polanyi virtually writes a history of the world and life on pp. 387–89) we can see that the rise of living individuals "overcome[s] the meaningless of the universe by establishing in it centres of subjective interests." Then "the rise of human thought in its turn overcame these subjective interests, by its universal intent." This enabled man as a living creature to develop ideas and a culture that can transcend, in terms of meaning, his mortality, in which he belongs with the animals.

This anthropogenesis is unspecifiable in terms of the inanimate particulars, for no events according to the laws of physics and chemistry can be conscious. No scientific account on material lines, whether in terms of classical mechanics or quantum mechanics can give an account of human consciousness. Darwinism can give no account of the descent of man, because evolution can only be understood as a feat of emergence. What we have to investigate (as E. W. F. Tomlin stresses) is the dynamics we are forced to call intelligence or primary consciousness in "life."

Polanyi's conclusion is breath-taking in the responsibility it lands us with. It could be that our capacity to know is an achievement that the universe has been striving to bring about, but that may exist only in us:

> So far as we know, the tiny fragments of the universe embodied in man are the only centres of thought and responsibility in the visible world. If that be so, the appearance of the human mind has been so far the ultimate stage in the awakening of the world; and all that has gone before, the strivings of a myriad centres that have taken the risks of living and believing, seem to have all been pursuing, along rival lines the aim now achieved by us at this point. (*PK*, p. 405)

They have all been quests for "ultimate liberation."

This account leaves out a great deal in Polanyi, about politics, history and religion, but I have tried to delineate his reconsideration of *what knowing is and what it involves,* to show that he requires us, by implication, to reconsider all our attitudes to ourselves and to the world. Whether we agree with him or not, and whether or not we agree with his disciple Marjorie Grene, we must surely be deeply aware of the limitations of the "objective" view, of positivism, and especially of the impress of these scientific dogmas on the humanities and the modern arts. As Polanyi says in his last book, *Meaning*, written in collaboration with Harry Prosch.

> modern science cannot properly be understood to tell us that the world is meaningless and pointless, that it is absurd. The supposition that it is absurd is a modern myth, created imaginatively from the clues produced by a profound misunderstanding of what science and knowledge are and what they require, a misunderstanding spawned by positivistic left-overs in our thinking and by allegiance to the false ideal of objectivity from which we have been unable to shake ourselves quite free. These are the stoppages in our ears that we must pull out if we are ever once more to experience the full range of meanings possible to man. (*Meaning*, p. 181)

Polanyi urges us to seek to live in a society in which men can be respected and honored as creators and bearers of such meanings. If we cannot achieve this, we may find ourselves involved in some collective process of stamping out these meanings on the grounds of some supposed social utility or some overpowering cause. Even in the supposedly open and civilized context of a university, one finds intense dogmatic resistance in the name of positivism to radical ideas that challenge its limitations, and some heretics report that while colleagues privately express their sympathy after public lectures, most will not join them openly out of fear of being punished, of being refused for posts, or of being refused research support. The context in which the debate goes on, in the quest to recognize the subjective realities of life and the existential nature of knowledge, is already one in which the enemies of dialogue are active, and show themselves as no great friends of freedom or devotees of Socratic dialogue and the pursuit of truth.

In the humanities, there is an urgent need for us to examine the implicit sense that, under the impress of positivist thinking, man's moral achievements seem to have no place in the world as delineated by modern science, as Polanyi points out. Despite the great authority of science, its "criteria of objectivity must deny reality to any moral claims" (Polanyi). As we know, there are moral problems, even if science cannot find them. What shall we say of probity? As Polanyi dryly puts it,

> No chemical analysis or microscopic examination can prove that a man who bears false witness is immoral. (*Knowing and Being,* p. 46)

So we must neither allow science to deny ethical values, nor allow science to declare that we must find answers to our moral problems in scientific or even "rational" findings alone. Of course, in our choices and actions, and in ethics as a theory and discipline, we need to take account of the *findings* of science, and to be rational. But since scientific findings can be argued only from empirical induction, they cannot be the whole basis of moral conclusions. Moral conclusions must be reached by the disciplines of ethics, and humanities subjects related to Ethics, which are capable of concerning themselves with the phenomena of consciousness.

But here, of course, we may have to struggle to get the most evident realities recognized. Some scientists in the past like Hebb have declared that "the existence of something called consciousness is a venerable hypothesis: not a datum, not directly observable."

So, the first step is to insist on a *holistic* approach to man, who must be regarded both as an organism and as a *being*, with a subjective life and consciousness.

As Polanyi points out, the wider problems (and the wider absurdities) are to be explained in terms of the threat that the recognition of consciousness manifests to science:

> Neurologists, like all the rest of us, know the difference between consciousness and unconsciousness; when they deny it, they mean that, since it eludes explanations in terms of science, *its existence endangers science,* and must be denied in the interests of science. (*Knowing and Being,* p. 42, emphasis added)

Because of this, there is even an absurdity in reductionist science, born of fear and obscurantism. Those who believe in evolution by selection must assume that consciousness is useful, since if it hadn't been, it would have been selected out. But since all bodily processes must be explained by physics and chemistry, the scientist cannot admit that consciousness can set a living body in motion. This contradiction, Polanyi says, is not, as far as he knows, ever examined in scientific debate. He quotes a neurologist who jumped up and down at a conference and shouted, "One thing we do know—ideas don't move muscles!"

So, consciousness, if it exists, can only be assumed to be strictly ineffectual. It cannot be fitted into evolutionary theory and so must be excluded from scientific recognition. This, says Polanyi, indicates doubletalk, in scientists who demonstrate every hour of their working day that they are impelled by passion, faith, belief, and so on—not least in asserting an "objectivity" that excludes all these, and passionately arguing against recognition of the consciousness that impels them.

Polanyi distinguishes between "attending to" (i.e., looking "at" the amoeba) and "attending from"—which is a way of *"dwelling in"* the amoeba by projecting oneself into it, imaginatively—the imaginative act involving one in feeling about the "insideness" of the amoeba in terms of how one feels from the inside of one's own body. Those spatial concepts owe a great deal to the French phenomenologist Merleau-Ponty, and the new feeling in philosophical biology about looking at living things involves us in realizing that it is only "by making intelligent use of our body" that we know ourselves to be in the body and not a thing outside, while our body is also the "ultimate instrument of all our external knowledge." In recognizing a face or exploring a problem we are "attending from" our whole complex of body and mind, so that we can be said to be "dwelling in" the phenomena we observe. This raises questions of the "tacit" or unseen and explicit aspects of knowing, and also a different view of what we see (when we look at a living being) and how we see it.

We may take the first step toward philosophical revolution by looking at an amoeba, as one might in a science lesson. In terms of the "conceptual recovery" necessary for the revolution needed in our thoughts we need to see that there is "another" way of looking at the amoeba. This way is as yet exceedingly difficult for us to grasp, because we are so conditioned, even by school science, to look at things in those "laboratory" ways which prevent us from seeing their wholeness, and the essential indivisibility, in universe and observer, of the creative dynamics of life as it exists and develops. To grasp this "new" way we need new concepts and terms.

Here are the clearest indications of the need to change paradigms. The "objective" psychologist can only preserve his paradigm if he carefully refuses to become aware of what the philosophical biologist can see—the delicate and subtle interaction, in both animals and man, between body-life and meaning, mutual encounter, and perception. A new emphasis is being placed on the mysterious and marvelous realities of perception, our "centricity" and autonomy, and the way in which our seeing creates the world.

In the ethical sphere, inevitably, the discovery of our involvement in knowing opens up new moral issues. As Polanyi says, knowing is an act that involves us in value and meaning. It has been a disaster that knowledge has, as in some strict science, become separated from awareness of man's moral being, because this is the kind of reality empiricism cannot "find." Knowledge of participation, as firmly grounded, Polanyi says, makes a clean sweep of the claim that in order to be valid, knowledge must be established objectively, without relying on personal judgment. And this restores our confidence in moral principles that are ultimately "known to us by our commitment to them."[8] In his *Personal Knowledge* as we have seen, Polanyi demonstrated that all knowledge is rooted in the participation of whole persons, so that science, for instance, is something that *scientists are doing,* that men are doing—and it is not only false but immoral ever to support that there is some body of "objective" truth to which we must defer, or that can absolve us from participation in moral issues, values, and meaning.

Polanyi is bold enough to say that the problem is not that of misunderstandings of the scientific world view, but that destructiveness of a kind is the very essence of the scientific outlook:

For what I am attacking is a claim of science that is even more deep-seated than the ideal of explaining everything in terms of the world's atomic topography. Long before Laplace formulated the atomic theory of the universe, science has accepted the ideal of strict objectivity and claimed that its results were strictly detached, impersonal. . . . I have shown now that this claim is unreasonable and that its pursuit obscures the very essence of human existence. The facts of a stratified universe can be known to science only by a personal participation of the scientist and this alone offers the grounds for securing moral values from destruction by a strictly objectivist analysis. ("Science and Man," p. 975)

While there is no call for us to be hostile to science, it is important to recognize that there have been dangers in the way in which science has contributed to "objective detachment" from values, because of misunderstandings of what science implies, and of the nature of thought and truth. Once we grasp the commitment and participation of man as scientist, and the subjective basis of scientific discovery, then the way is open to restore values to the pursuit of truth.

Notes

1. "The Scientific Fallacy," *Encounter* (November 1969), p. 59.
2. Cf. W. I. B. Beveridge, *The Art of Scientific Investigation,* which has chapters on *Imagination* and *Intuition* (London: Heinemann, 1950). This is an introductory training book for young research scientists.
3. Yet in conversation with leading microbiologist Dr. Sidney Brenner, the Nobel prize-winner, I gathered that this phrase meant absolutely nothing to him at all. See *Evolution and the Humanities.*
4. See "The Recognition of Species" in *Science Progress* 42 (1957): 587. Pantin used to tell his students "Bring in any worms that sneer at you," thus indicating the subjective element in the process of species recognition.
5. Horace Freeland Judson, *The Eighth Day of Creation, The Makers of the Revolution in Biology* (London: Jonathan Cape, 1979).
6. See Paul Weiss, *Principles of Development. A Text in Experimental Embryology.* (New York: U. Holt and Co., 1939). See also Weiss's contribution to he *Alpbach Seminar,* ed. Koestler and Smithies (London: Hutchinson, 1969).
7. See Kurt Goldstein, *Human Nature in the Light of Psychopathology* (Cambridge: Harvard University Press, 1940).
8. "Science and Man," *Proceedings of the Royal Society of Medicine* 58 (1970): 975.

7
Values and Ethical Living: E. K. Ledermann and Other Existentialist Views

The rejection of the mechanistic paradigm, and its metaphysical effects on us, at least leaves us with a sense that there is no need for us to accept that there is nothing we can believe in. If we note the absurdity of mind looking at the world and declaring it meaningless, this helps. So it does if we note that there does seem to be a need to introduce some teleological element into our thinking, and recognize something like an "innovative principle" in the cosmos, and see a gradient in nature. If we recognize that there are "protensions" in our relationship to time, and see ourselves as the "upsurge of time," then perhaps we may sense that life in the world and our own existence are far more mysterious than we have so far realized, even far more mysterious than most religions have so far believed.

However, this does not add up to the possibility of a positive "belief," nor solve the problem of the grounds for meaning and values: we cannot have hymns to "gradients" or "protensions." But at least we need not feel paralyzed, as if by an array of "scientific facts" with which we cannot argue. At least we can say to ourselves there is no cause in the present state of knowledge to believe that the world is meaningless and that man's life is without meaning or value. And, moreover, we can also recognize that we "know the kind of work that has to be done," as Abraham Maslow has put it.

As the participants declared at the conference on values discussed in Maslow's *New Knowledge in Human Values*, humanists have for years been trying to construct a naturalistic, psychological value system from man's own nature. Today it is possible for the first time to feel confident that this age-old hope may be fulfilled.

As we have seen, a good deal of relevant thinking has been going on in the realm of psychotherapy. Philosophical anthropology has placed strong emphasis on the natural capacity of man to be moral, and an important theme in existentialist thinking is the nature of moral freedom.

Psychotherapeutic observation comes to show that there is a continual struggle in the human soul, between true and false self, and true and false meanings. The struggle between love and hate, between the true and the false, between authenticity and inauthenticity, must be seen as part of a fundamental struggle in man that "belongs" to his nature. Our goal is the discovery and release of that which is truly felt to be authentic in us, in the service of our life tasks. But because man is free, in the existentialist sense, he can define himself and choose his destiny. Of course, it is possible for him to choose the false, to base his modes of dealing with the world on hate and moral inversion, even if this threatens his survival. Because of the advances of technological power, mankind can now, quite clearly, choose to end human life on earth. But I believe that by its penetration into psychotherapy, existentialism has developed beyond its view in some hands, that all attempts to define oneself are futile and absurd. Even under the influence of the gloomy philosophy of Martin Heidegger and such concepts of being-unto-death, such movements as *Daseinsanalysis* have generated a sense that there can be genuine answers to the problem of life.

How can man work on the problem of avoiding false choices and the sense of futility and meaninglessness? There do seem to be sources of truth about human nature to which we must pay responsible attention. To bring about his own destruction, as Polanyi argues, would mark the ultimate failure of man to accept the responsibility given to him as the conscious knower. So, one of the deepest problems in our life is to accept the burden of knowledge, in the recognition that man is, as far as we know, the only bearer of the capacity to *know*. And since knowing is inevitably bound up with values, with the moral responsibilities knowledge brings, to know and to be moral are to be human.

The seminar on humanistic values, *New Knowledge in Human Values,* to which I have referred above, may be related to Abraham Maslow's emphases in his own work, *Towards A Psychology of Being.* Maslow's book is an attempt to correct psychology, and especially psychoanalysis, by pointing to the fact that too much of it has concerned itself with sickness. Attention to healthy psychology reveals more creativity. In normal people there are transcendent moments that add a quality to life that makes it specifically a *mode of being* rather than simply *existing.* These *are* biological realities. Life has a meaning for human beings and they experience "peak moments" during which the significance and uniqueness of their lives seem confirmed. Indeed, it seems clear that man cannot live without this sense and, of course, it indicates realms of creative or intentional experience too often missing from traditional psychology and sociology. But in discussing his own book, in the latter chapters Maslow speaks of his difficulties in getting over the whole question of "the

cute or poignant problem of our identity-existence." This, he found, was
gain a matter of paradigms:

> We are groping . . . towards the phenomenological, the experiential, the
> existential, the ideographic, the unconscious, the private, the acutely
> personal; but it has become clear to me that we are trying to do this in
> an inherited intellectual atmosphere or framework which is quite un-
> suitable and unsympathetic, one which I might even call forbidding.
> (*TB*, p. 316)

The "forbidding" nature of this atmosphere has now become an actual
ntolerance. Our journals, books, and conferences, he says, are primarily
uitable for the communication and discussing of the rational, the abstract,
ne logical, the public, the impersonal, the homothetic, the repeatable, the
bjective, and the unemotional:

> They therefore assume the very things that we "personal psychologists"
> are trying to change. In other words, they beg the question. One result is
> that as therapists or self-observers we are still forced by academic
> custom to talk about our experiences or those of patients in about the
> same way as we might talk about bacteria, or about the moon, or about
> white rats, *assuming* that we are detached, distant and uninvolved,
> *assuming* that we (and the objects of perception) are unmoved and
> unchanged by the act of observation must be cool and never warm,
> *assuming* that cognition can only be contaminated or distorted by
> emotion, etc. (*TB*, p. 216)

Iaslow demands attention to the nonlogical, the poetic, the mythic, the
igue, the primary processes, the dreamlike. We might say (following
tern, Guntrip, and Winnicott) that he is asking for greater attention to the
feminine" modes:

> We must help the "scientific" psychologists to realise that they are
> working on the basis of a philosophy of science, and that any philoso-
> phy of science which serves primarily an excluding function is a set of
> blinders, a handicap rather than a help. *All* the world, all of experience
> must be open to study. Nothing, not even the "personal" problem need
> be closed off from human investigation. . . . I am suggesting that we
> enlarge the jurisdiction of science so as to include within its realm the
> problems and data of personal and experiential psychology.

s philosophical biology discovers that man is primarily a symbolizing
iimal, then it must assume that this symbolizing energy has a function.
his function will not in any satisfactory biology be judged in terms of
evolution" alone, but as something to do with human survival in the
idest sense. One of the possibilities is that by using his symbolizing

functions man may come to discover both a greater sense of responsibilit' to the forces of life in the universe and a greater freedom. Nothing coul be less free than not surviving! Philosophical biology is the study of livin; creatures in this wider perspective, and what is involved is nothing les than a new view of man's place in the scheme of things.

As Maslow says, science itself, insofar as it sticks to "objectivity," ma actually be a form of avoiding the whole truth:

> Looking for order, law, control, predictability, graspability in the star and plants is often isomorphic with the search for *inner* law, control, etc Impersonal science can sometimes be a flight from or defence agains inner order and chaos, against the fear of loss of control. Or, to put i more generally, impersonal science can be (and often enough is, I hav found) a flight from or defence against the personal within oneself o within other human beings a distaste for emotions and impulse, eve sometimes a disgust with humanness or a fear of it. (*TB*, p. 237)

We in the humanities ought surely to counteract this trend away fror human life toward detachment, and to insist on the fullness of life an experience in the pursuit of moral freedom.

What 'moral freedom' means, in any sphere of life, as well as in psycho therapy, is the subject of Dr. E. K. Ledermann's book on existentia psychotherapy, *Neurosis as a Moral Phenomenon*. Here Ledermann dis cusses several existentialists—Frankl, Husserl, Jaspers, Rollo May, an Buber, in relation to psychotherapy. His remarks can be applied to educa tion, if we conceive of it as *education for being*.

Jung is quoted as saying, "About a third of my cases are suffering fror clinically definable neurosis, but from the senselessness and emptiness c their lives." Frankl confirms Jung's view that this kind of suffering is th "general neurosis of our time":

> To Frankl, "this striving to find a meaning in one's life is . . . regarded a the primary motivational force in man."

Ledermann quotes D. R. A. McInnes, whose patients were Oxfor undergraduates who displayed a "persistent feeling of pointlessness an futility":

> These students were unable to organize their lives or to establish goa towards which they might move. Their affective state had been likene to that of early schizophrenia but they were certainly not schizophreni and did not become so. (*EN*, p. 27)

McInnes said that this phenomenon was of more than medical interes indeed, it seems obviously of interest to the humanities and education i general. These young people demanded a "credo" from the doctor, who concluded that "this therapeutic situation epitomized the challenge of our time."

A similar observation is made by Frankl in his *Psychotherapy and Existentialism:* he says that psychoanalysts report a new kind of neurosis in today's world characterized by loss of interest and lack of initiative.

Time and again the psychiatrist is consulted by patients who *doubt that life has any meaning.* This condition I have called "existential vacuum."

Frankl refers to a statistical survey made among his students. In the University of Vienna, only 40% of the students (German, Swiss, and Austrian) who attended his lectures said that they knew from their own experience the *feeling of absolute absurdity.* Among American students the figure was 81%. He concludes that the "existential vacuum" is a *concomitant of industrialization;* and, of course, since Frankl's time, we have, in industrial society, suffered a great deal more from economic difficulties, which no one seems to be able to understand, let alone solve.

Ledermann refers to Karl Mannheim's *Diagnosis of Our Time,* (London: Routledge and Kegan Paul, 1945) in which the sociologist asks why so many people feel life to be pointless and futile. Mannheim suggests that this is because their lives are planned too much. The many measures of social control necessary for our kind of society take away people's volition. Even efficiency, says Ledermann, "creates a pathology of boredom," while technology has deprived the individual of "intimate participation in the creative activities of his group" (Dubos). We have acquired the economic power to own things, but they are anonymously produced. (To this, of course, we need to add today the even greater contribution to meaninglessness that unemployment makes.)

Anonymity and lack of opportunities for creative activities are intolerable, says Ledermann, for men's self-respect and dignity. Yet what about leisure, for this surely has been increased? Here, however, we suffer from a mechanistic industrialization of leisure. (See E. W. F. Tomlin "Positive and Negative Nutrition" in *Psyche, Culture, and the New Science.*) In countries where technological advance has been highest, we have the highest rates of drug addiction, alcoholism, suicide, and social violence. (In France in the early eighties suicide has been said to be the major cause of death in the 16–25 age group.) In many areas of our life men find themselves in a "spiritual desert."

Ledermann quotes Mannheim again, who says that people are not only suffering from a lack of opportunities to "express themselves," but much more from an uncertainty of values that could guide them in their expression.

In a society where disintegration has proceeded too far, the paradoxical situation arises that education, social work and propaganda . . . become less and less efficient because all values that could guide them tend to evaporate. (*Diagnosis of Our Time*, 1945)

Today it is even worse, for while education is expected to uphold values, it can hardly be supposed to succeed when the public at large is conditioned by a hedonistic and trivial culture.

Ledermann's quotations from Mannheim are therefore immediately relevant to education:

What is the use of developing exceedingly skilful methods . . . new techniques of learning . . . if we do not know what they are for? What is the good of developing child guidance, psychiatric social work and psychotherapy if the one who is to guide is left without standards? Sooner or later everyone becomes neurotic, as it gradually becomes impossible to make a reasonable choice in the chaos of competing and unreconciled valuations. (*EN*, p. 28)

This was written in 1942, and it makes plain the similarity between problems in education and those in psychotherapy. Mannhein was seeking social causes, and indeed there are many causes of our unsettledness—conflicts of social values that can become unbearable:

Christianity versus Marxist materialism, craftmanship versus mass production, obedience as a principle in education versus freedom of expression; authority in government versus *laissez-faire*—these are some of the major antagonisms which he identified. (*EN*, p. 29)

It is true that a change in social norms and in ideologies can be unsettling when people lose faith in themselves. In such case they may prove not strong enough to stand alone. But

the ultimate test is whether man can discover his moral strength to deal with his challenge. (*EN*, p. 28)

Ledermann then makes a brief survey of certain ethical philosophies. Some writers deny the theoretical values of any moral standards. Others base their ethical system on secular humanism. M. T. Hindson postulates an ethical system based on the "logic of feeling," which would fulfill itself in "unselfish behavior." But, says Ledermann, the feelings are illogical, so his system is impossible. L. L. Whyte seems to believe that a system could be based on scientific rationalism, since science cannot find such intangibles as wisdom in soundness of judgment, or an intelligent moral sense. Again, an ethical system cannot be based on objective disciplines—only on subjective ones. There is no unified science of man, among all the "objective" disciplines that science displays, on which to base an ethical system.

Some rationalist humanists seek to base their ethic on planning for happiness and efficiency for all, as does Erich Fromm.[1] Humanistic conscience is knowledge within oneself, knowledge of our respective success and failure in the act of living.

Happiness for Fromm is to be achieved through "productiveness." But this, says Ledermann, is still hedonistic, even though not based merely on the pursuit of pleasure.

The linking of ethics with happiness, says Ledermann, is a fallacy:

A moral action produces the satisfaction of a good conscience, but a man cannot achieve a good conscience if he aims at the feeling of self-satisfaction through his actions. The neurotic whose life feels empty may try desperately to fill it with pleasure and happiness, but his efforts will be in vain. (*EN*, p. 32)

Joan Austin has pointed out that what is needed, more than happiness, is a "total condition in which man feels safe."[2] Ledermann goes on,

happiness cannot be procured through scientific knowledge and . . . the unhappiness of the neurotic who experiences his life as meaningless cannot be relieved by a faith constructed in a rational manner out of scientific concepts. (*EN*, p. 32)

Science can therefore never be a religion, nor can it be the basis for a genuine education of the spirit or moral capacity toward existential security.

Ledermann next turns to Viktor Frankl's "ontological value ethics," which he finds much more congenial since it is based on an existentialist position. Frank's account of human existence "attempts an analysis in the ontological sense . . . an unfolding of the essence of personal existence." Frankl believes that, in the sphere of the somatic and the psychic, man is governed by the principle of determinism; physical disorders can bring psychic disturbance, and in the psychic field there are to be found the "drives"—for Freud the "will-to-pleasure"; for Adler the "will-to-power."

But Frankl adds a third dimension, that of freedom and values. "It is here," says Ledermann, "that man is expected to transcend himself and to find meaning in his life." The "logotherapist" who follows Frankl's path

makes [this patient] aware of the hidden *logos* in his existence thus enabling him to fill his existential vacuum which, according to Frankl, is manifest in the "mass neurosis of the present time," a form of nihilism which is defined as "the contention that being has no meaning." (*EN*, p. 33)

The values toward which the patient is to be led are (a) the creative values realized when a task is achieved; (b) the experiential values, which are brought about when the Beautiful, the Good or the True are experienced or the single human being is perceived in his uniqueness in a loving relationship; and (c) the attitudinal values that result from "the very attitude in which we face our destined suffering . . . an achievement of meaning through suffering . . . when the suffering is unavoidable and unacceptable."[3]

Ledermann discusses Frankl's therapeutic techniques of "paradoxical intention" and "de-reflexion." Perhaps these may free a patient from troublesome symptoms, but there is still a need to put more emphasis on achieving a meaningful existence, for a meaningful existence is *not* a mere freedom from symptoms of anxiety and compulsion. (As we have seen, Winnicott says, "You may cure your patient and not know what it is that makes him or her go on living. . . . absence of psycho-neurotic illness may be health, but it is not life" [*Playing and Reality,* p. 100].)

Frankl argues that not every neurosis is the result of a conflict affecting concience or values. But Ledermann is not happy about Frankl's division of problems into sexual neuroses, which require Freudian scientific treatment to deal with the "will-to-pleasure," superiority-complex neuroses, which need the Adlerian deterministic approach to cope with the "will-to-power," and "noögenic"[4] neuroses, which qualify for Frankl's logotherapy, based on the "will-to-meaning."

Ledermann believes it is wrong to put these three "wills" side by side, since each could seem to belong to a different model. The will-to-meaning is the overall will and represents the essence of the existential approach. The others represent challenges of different kinds that cannot be coordinated. The sexual will is the instinctual desire that can bring a person into conflict within his "spiritual dimension" unless sexual attraction coincides with love. The will-to-power is a neurotic will that inevitably comes into conflict with the "loving relationship" between people.

Adler wanted the "will to power" (or "masculine protest") suppressed; Freud believed the will-to-sexual-pleasure should be given more expression. Neither solution reaches the real problem, but it is impossible to treat sexual power and noögenic problems as if they were separate. Ledermann aims at

> their confrontation with the particular person's conscience so that he can come to terms with the conscious and unconscious demands of these potent volitional forces and can achieve a meaningful existence by integrating them with his realm of values. (*EN,* p. 36)

This seems to me to be a much better existentialist position. Ledermann declares that existential ethics must avoid a number of pitfalls. The existentialist ethic seeks to enable contemporary man to overcome his moral crisis in the personal, unique self: this ethic implies the recognition of values as they are created and experienced by the self. The pitfalls are:

1. The self must not be divorced from ethical principles.
2. Self-realization does not mean that the self, left to itself, realizes itself. People need a philosophy that calls for an effort of transcending themselves to gain personal freedom.
3. Existential ethics are menaced by a deterministic psychology that postulates that the self is knowable as a measurable, fixed entity.

Ledermann invokes Jaspers, who said that to the "scientific objective cognition . . . there is no such thing as freedom." We can become familiar with freedom but we cannot know it in a defined concept. Yet conceptual activity is an achievement of the striving for freedom, as we have seen.

Although our knowledge will always contain a "maze of misconceptions," the movement of thought itself, reflection, is the manifestation of personal freedom that releases us. It provides:

a release from the obscure bondage of the indifferentiated, from the given thus-ness of the self *(Sosein)* from the power of uncritically accepted symbols and from the absolute reality of the objective world. (Jaspers, *General Psychopathology,* p. 348)

Ledermann refers to Jasper's term about developing outward and inward perception: *meaningful connections.*

Ledermann quotes, "To exist is to take leave of what one is *(ex)* in order to establish oneself *(sistere)* on the level which formerly was only possible." This points to a quest for authenticity and the transcendence of the personal self, in terms close to those used by Rollo May in his *Love and Will.*

Existential writers, however, as Ledermann points out, do not agree on the meanings of the words *authenticity* and *transcendence.* Ledermann is disappointed with Rollo May for, although he seems to give a satisfactory account of authenticity, he also seems to suggest that transcendence is achieved only by rare people—saints and great creative figures. Ledermann, like Abraham Maslow, believes that transcendence is available to all. Indeed, Maslow believed that the continual everyday experience of peak moments was what kept every normal individual satisfied, with a feeling that these gave meaning and purpose to his life.

Anyone who has taught in a creative way must surely touch or find a glimpse every now and then of the quest for *authenticity* that lies at the heart of every human being.

Bugental sees authenticity as "being in the world . . . unqualifiedly in accord with the givenness of his own nature and the world."[5] Transcendence, to Bugental, is the emergence beyond "full authenticity of being" into "oneness with the All." "By its nature it partakes of mystery or mysticism. . . . transcendence is complete awareness and full feelingful assent." "But the kind of person who can achieve this," says Bugental, would be

> a very different person [from] most of us, somewhat difficult for us to communicate with, and rather frightening to know.

As Ledermann says, both Rollo May and Bugental seem to offer a kind of transcendence that is beyond the reach of most people. It is true that the "formative principle" in each human being, the quest for authenticity, is a mystery; but our philosophy of life suffers if we fail to recognize that this mystery is there in every person. Winnicott's work reveals it to be a mystery, a mysterious achievement, for every child to develop the "I AM" feeling: and every child is compelled to ask those question, "What is it to be human?" and "What is the point of life?"

Culture, as a meeting point between the individual, the other, and the world of ideas and causes beyond the self, is the vehicle of transcendence. For (as Jaspers said) if man is to maintain his inner integrity in the face of fate and death, "he cannot do so by himself alone."

> What helps him here is of a different kind from any help in the world. Transcendent help reveals itself to him solely in the fact that he can be himself. That he can stand by himself, he owes to an intangible hand, extended to him from transcendence, a hand whose presence he can feel only in his freedom. (Jaspers, *The Perennial Scope of Philosophy,* pp. 64–65)

Transcendence is a "basic trait" in man's consciousness, in his inner world, Jasper believes.

Ledermann then turns to Husserl's phenomenology. He called the relationship between the self and his experience "intentional,"

> by which he meant that data of consciousness cannot be separated from the self, but that the self sends out a 'shaft of attention' which terminates in the object of consciousness. There is no empty consciousness, only consciousness with contents which are the experiences and 'the bearers of specific quality of intentionality' such as colour, touch, sound, pleasure, pain, and a feeling of animation. (*EN,* p. 41[6])

Husserl's view of man in the world does not conceive the realm of experience as something passive and unalterable, but on the contrary, as something that the individual self has brought about consciously or unconsciously, and that he has the freedom to change.

Intentionality is preconscious, and Husserl postulated "a fringe of background inattention showing relative difference of clearness and obscurity." Through making the self aware of this background, we bring obscure areas into the full light of attention and become free to change the world of our experience.

Intentionality thus belongs to those deeper areas of existence with which the poet is familiar, and which the child displays in creative work. Here Ledermann turns to Merleau-Ponty, who explored the stage before we can formulate our thoughts and knowledge of the world. Quoting Husserl, Merleau-Ponty called this important activity "operative intentionality" and characterized it as

> that which produces the natural and antepredicative unity of the world and of our life, being apparent in our desires, our evalutions and in the landscape we see, more clearly than in objective knowledge, and furnishing the text which our knowledge tried to translate into precise language. (*Phenomenology of Perception*, p. xviii)

This sentence alone has immense implications for education, for in creative work it is just this penumbra of being-in-the-world, before we are able to speak of it, with which we are dealing.[7] By becoming aware of this operative intentionality, by "realizing his freedom towards his inner world," which he can alter to some extent, "man realizes his freedom in relation to his outer world," says Ledermann.

In Husserl's philosophy, the outer world is "put into brackets": he was not concerned with reality as such, but with man's consciousness of it. But freedom demands that we recognize our responsibilities to a reality that is undeniably "there." Here Ledermann turns to Buber's philosophy, and his distinction between the I-Thou and the I-It, the latter being a dimension in which man can be dealt with "without any feeling for their exclusiveness." So "he who lives with It alone is not a man," and the question arises of man's nullification in our thought. In this distinction alone there is a profound criticism of our society and civilization (and much of our educational thought—as in much sociology). Too much in our culture belongs too much to the It, to a public It-ness that conveys a certain nihilism, and so does too much of our thought, not least in educational "research": it is deficient in ontology, the proper study of *being*.

Man is in need of the world of the Thou ("Through the Thou a man becomes I"). He becomes confirmed in his selfhood by another self in the I-Thou relationship. As we have seen, this is an "ethical principle" confirmed by the psychoanalysis of Winnicott, the philosophical biology of Buytendijk and Plessner, and the existentialism of Binswanger and May. It is a serious criticism of Sartre's kind of existentialism that he could see interpersonal relationships only as menacing—damaging in the sense of threatening one with "objectivity" and the denial of one's being. This simply does not accord with our experience. A similar failure is to be found in Marxism. As John Macmurray says, criticizing Marxism, it is the transcendence of the I-Thou relationship that Marxism fails to recognize sufficiently; for as Ledermann says, "although the Thou appears in space and in time, the I-Thou relationship is lived independently of the space-time coordinates":

> Let Rome in Tiber melt
> Here is my space. . . .

The freedom that is bound up with the transcendence man finds in the I-Thou relationship is lost if the "inborn *Thou*" does not meet a *Thou* in the outer world.[8]

Objects like a tree or an animal may speak to man as a Thou, but the I-Thou relationship is mostly between man and man. The I-Thou relationship, however, is always deteriorating, says Ledermann, into an I-It relationship: "It is the exalted melancholy of our fate that every *Thou* in the world must become an *It*." (Buber, *I and Thou*). In any relationship, people tend at times to treat one another as objects of which they can make use. In extremis, the functional view of man lends itself to a morality that sees the other as only there for use, which is the posture celebrated in the egotistical nihilism of Max Stirner.[9] But quite positive relationships and love not only confirm people in their being, but release potentialities. As Mary Midgley says in *Beast and Man*, "to rely on other people is not some kind of shameful weakness: it is an aspect of the need to be true to oneself"; dependence is a contribution to one's authenticity. It is up to persons in relationships to continually rebuild the I-Thou relationship and never take each other for granted.

> The I-Thou relationship requires two whole people to conduct the genuine dialogue in which "each should regard his partner as the very one he is," accepting him and confirming him as a partner. (*EN*, p. 43)

It may be that the present age is not conducive to the development of the I-Thou relationship, as Ledermann points out, quoting Buber and Jaspers. To make another into an "It" is to make him into something that is "not a man," and this is the objection to the debasement and dehumanization that are flagrant in our society, both in commercialism and in much of today's fashionable radicalism.[10] Here may be forms of blasphemy to human dignity and freedom. "The 'mystery' of the interhuman life," says Ledermann, "is destroyed by the scientific-analytical attitude which objectifies the psyche" (ibid.). Many psychotherapists are concerned with the effects of scientific-analytical approaches to the psychic life that dehumanize people, in thought or practice (see especially Jan

Foudraine, *Not Made of Wood* and the work of Peter Lomas, as in *True and False Experience*).

Much of the nature of our life today, with its restless, manic activity, with streams of cars continually buzzing along concrete roadways, huge blank buildings dominating the individuals below them, insensitive living and working conditions that depersonalize us, and an industrialized culture that does the same—all these influences tend to destroy the mystery of the creative intercourse between men about which Buber writes so beautifully. Our work in the humanities cannot but be impelled to be a contribution to the defense of creative being in this dehumanizing world.

Ledermann places an emphasis, as we do in creative work in English, not only on communicating but on communicating with oneself, on the inward dialogue in the quest for meaning. Then there is the dialogue between this self, the voice of our innermost needs and the inner area of being where "ethical living" has its roots, and "society."

Many sociologists idolize "society" as an entity greater than the individual, but according to Albert Schweitzer, "society has no claim to lay down ethics for the individual." He said:

> The collapse of civilization has come through ethics being left to society. . . . A renewal . . . is possible only if ethics become once more the concern of thinking human beings, and if individuals seek to assert themselves in society as ethical personalities. (*Civilisation and Ethics,* p. 262)

Ledermann places emphasis on existential guilt, which comes when someone evades his personal duty, when he fails to make the right use of his potentialities, when he wastes his life. He quotes Buber, who said that guilt occurs when someone injures an order of the human world whose foundations he knows and recognizes as those of his own existence and of all common human existence.[11] Conscience makes us conscious of our tasks in life. The most important aspect of existentialism is its protest against all those accumulating forces that tend in our time to dehumanize man. Its most hopeful aspect is the rejection of "the public"—that collectivization which (to use Buber's word) *nullifies* man. The "public," said Kierkegaard, is "nothing more than an artificial agglomeration of individuals—a fairy story in an age of understanding." Heidegger discussed the loss of authenticity in somewhat different terms. He declares that living merely like others is an inauthentic mode of existence, a denial of man's essential nature. In existentialist thought man is urged to claim and exert his uniqueness. Kierkegaard offered us two alternatives:

> *Either:* the life of the individual person, a microcosm of the image of God, capable of free, responsive action, and therefore . . . a life of toil

and . . . suffering . . . and danger: *or:* the life of an impersonal unfree member of a collective, without the possibility of independent knowledge and responsible action . . . and as compensation for the loss of freedom at best a false illusory dream of material welfare in an earthly paradise which can never become a reality. (K. F. Reinhardt, *The Existentialist Revolt* [Milwaukee: Bruce Publishing Co., 1952], p. 36)

We must begin to know by not knowing. This may seem a strange position for an educator to advocate. (See the excellent discussion in George F. Kneller, *Existentialism and Education,* 1958.) But this is the way out from both the illusory dream of material welfare *and* the "objective" paradigm in the philosophy of a materialist society. Both make us incapable of true joy, but also of the dread, doubt, and sense of mystery that belong to a true tragic sense of our predicament. Without these dimensions we remain uncreative, and the urgent "tragic" problem of the meaning of life is not faced. The failure to pursue the problem of meaning in life, the failure of intentionality, and our failure to find creative time belong to a failure of will. Rollo May who calls ours the "age of disordered will," diagnoses this failure of a creative will as a schizoid disease of our society:

My term "schizoid," in the title of this chapter, means *out of touch: avoiding close relationships: the inability to feel.* I do not use the term as a reference to psychopathology, but rather as a general condition of our culture and the tendencies of people which make it up. . . .
. . . the schizoid condition is a general tendency in our transitional age. (*LW,* p. 16)

The psychic casualties of our time, he says, are the products of parents and families who have become reduced to functional dimension, and are thus "unwitting expressions of their culture. The schizoid man is the natural product of the technological man" (*LW,* p. 17).

A number of existentialist writers have pointed to this mechanical passivity in people's lives today. A combination of a social system that reduces people to their functions with a philosophy that justifies this has led people to think of themselves in terms of "functional man," says Gabriel Marcel. Marjorie Grene delineates the passivity of mind that has resulted from our imprisonment in philosophy that sees the world as a world of dead objects. This passivity goes with a passivity before a world of technicism, as Rollo May argues. We are offered "power and freedom," but

a *passive* role is expected of the citizen who is to be recipient. Not only in the medium of advertising, but in matters of education, health, the drugs, things are done *to* and *for* us by the new inventions: our role, however subtly put, is to submit, accept the blessing, and be thankful. (*LW,* p. 186)

There are great technical achievements, like sending rockets to the moon; but you and I as individual persons have nothing whatever to do with such achievements except to pay our taxes through anonymous, labyrinthine channels and watch the space flights on television. The dilemma is sharpened, furthermore, by the fact that just when we fell most powerless in the face of the juggernaut of impersonal power that surrounds and molds us, we are called upon to take responsibility for much vaster and more portentous choices. Meanwhile,

> there is confusion approaching bankruptcy in outward guidance for sex by society, family, and church. The gift of freedom, yes; but the burden placed on the individual is tremendous indeed. (*LW,* p. 187)

Obviously, to escape from such a situation requires a major philosophical change, which involves recognition of the primacy of *feeling* and *care.* Rollo May returns to Kierkegaard:

> "In love every man starts from the beginning," wrote Søren Kierkegaard. This beginning is the relationship between people which we term care. Though it goes beyond feeling, it begins there. It is a feeling denoting a relationship of concern, when the other's existence matters to you; a relationship of dedication, taking the ultimate form of being willing to get delight in or, in ultimate terms, to suffer for, *the other.* (*LW,* p. 303, emphasis added)

Rollo May has a good deal to say about William James, to whom he traces the growing recognition in modern psychology of the primacy of feelings:

> The new basis for care is shown by the interest of psychologists and philosophers in emphasizing *feeling* as the basis of human existence. We now need to establish feeling as a legitimate aspect of our way of relation to reality. When William James says, "Feeling is everything," he means not that there is nothing *more* than feeling, but that everything starts there. Feeling commits one, ties one to the object, and ensures action. But in the decades after James made this "existentialist" statement, feelings became demoted and were disparaged as merely subjective. Reason or, more accurately, technical reason was the guide to the way issues were to be settled. We said "I feel" as a synonym for "I vaguely believe," when we didn't *know*—little realizing that we cannot *know* except as we *feel.* (*LW,* p. 303)

To many scientists "feeling" and "the subjective" are aspects of our response to the world that must be suppressed in their work, and generally regarded with suspicion; *subjective* is a perjorative word for them. In this, essentially, they are following the Galilean and Cartesian traditions, the deficiencies and dangers of which we have examined. Many thinkers now have a different principle on which to base their concepts of human relation. As May writes:

> The development of psychoanalysis has led to a resurgence of the primacy of feeling. And in academic psychology, a number of papers have come out lately that show the drift of psychologists and philosophers toward a new appreciation of feeling. Hadley Cantril's paper, *"Sentio, ergo sum,"* is one and Sylvan Tomkin's *"Homo patens"* is another. Susanne Langer entitles her new book, *Mind, An Essay on Feeling.* And Alfred North Whitehead, Miss Langer's teacher, in pointing out that Descartes was wrong in his principle, *Cogito, ergo sum,* goes on:
>
>> It is never bare thought or bare existence that we are aware of. I find myself rather as essentially a unity of emotion of enjoyment, of hopes, of fears, of regrets, valuations of alternatives, decisions—all of these are my subjective reactions to my environment as I am active in my nature. My unity which is Descartes' "I am" is my process of shaping this welter of material into a consistent *pattern of feeling.* (*LW,* pp. 303–4)[12]

As we have seen, Ernst Cassirer demands that we redefine man as the animal symbolicum. This new, unified man is one in whom we accept feelings, consciousness, meaning, love, and will. If we alter our model of man thus, there are, evidently, enormous educational implications.

Love, the emotional life, concern, and intentional will must be brought to the center of human studies. The realities of intersubjectivity and the related dynamics of creativity must be brought out in students themselves, not least by the concept they have of themselves. Like Rollo May, we must embrace the future:

> We love and will the world as an immediate, spontaneous totality. We *will* the world, create it by our decision, our fiat, our choice; and we *love* it, give it affect, energy, power to love us and change us as we mold and change it. This is what it means to be fully related to one's world. I would not imply that the world does not exist *before* we love or will it; one can answer that question only on the basis of his assumptions, and, being a mid-westerner with inbred realism, I would assume that it does exist. But I have no effect upon it; I move as in a dream, vaguely and without viable contact. One can choose to shut it out—as New Yorkers do when riding the subway—or one can choose to see it, create it. (Ibid., p. 324)

This involves us in a new approach to knowledge; we need a new kind of knowing, which is both *growledge* (to use Coleridge's word) and which creates the world as it is known:

> What does this mean concerning our personal lives to which, at last, we now return? The microcosm of our consciousness is where the mac-

rocosm of the universe is *known* . . . it is the curse of man that he can be conscious of himself and his world . . . Intentionality, itself consisting of the deepened awareness of one's self, is our means of putting the meaning surprised by consciousness into action. (Ibid., pp. 324–25)

With Viktor Frankl, May places an insistence on man's primary need for satisfactions of the will-to-meaning:

The meaning-matrix comes before any discussion, scientific or others, since it is what makes discussion—as in psychotherapy—possible. . . .

The same thing hold true in all human relationships so well:

. . . friendship and love require that we participate in the meaning-matrix of the other without surrendering our own. This is the way human consciousness understands, grows, changes, becomes clarified and meaningful. (*LW*, p. 262)

In therapy the problem is to get the patient to feel "I-am-the-one-who-has-these-wishes" and to become able to act in such a way that the whole being is involved in the act. In tackling the problems of education in our world it is the *meaning matrix* and the *involvement of the whole being* with which we must be concerned in order to heal schizoid dissociation.

Without confidence in our ability to *make* the future, we may never be able to escape from the paralysis into which our society has fallen, not from the desperate outburst of violence that troubles it. We know that in middle-class family life there is a kind of failure of values related to technology and the acquisitive society, which have related identity to "doing" and "manipulation":

It is a sound hypothesis, based on a good deal of evidence in psychotherapeutic work, that the unconscious guilt which parents . . . carry because they manipulate their children leads them to [be] over-protective and over-permissive toward the same. These are the children who are given motor cars but not moral values, who pick up sensuality but are not taught sensitivity in life. (*LW*, p. 278)

Mere "protest," as we have seen in recent decades, reaches no real answer. What is needed is deep study and experiment in new forms of living.[13]

A radical reconsideration of the way to solutions is needed—and this obviously needs a new approach to learning and education:

A final indication that the problem of love and will belong together is the similarity in their "solutions." Neither can be adequately dealt with in our day simply by new techniques, patching up the old values, restating old habits in more palatable form, or any other such device. We cannot content ourselves by painting the old building a new color; it is the foundations which are destroyed, and the "resolutions," by whatever name we may call them, require new ones.

What is necessary for "resolutions" is a new consciousness in which the depth and meaning of personal relationship will occupy a central place. Such an embracing consciousness is always required in an age of radical transition. Lacking external guides, we shift our morality inward; there is a new demand upon the individual of personal responsibility. *We are required to discover on a deeper level what it means to be human.* (*LW*, p. 279, emphasis added)

By saying "God is dead," May argues, "Nietzsche did not mean to promote amorality or nihilism." On the contrary, he was radically devoted, like Kierkegaard, to rejecting sick and dying, deteriorated forms of theism and emotionally dishonest religious practices. Nietzsche sought to promote the self-realization of the individual in the fullest sense—and this is what he meant by the "will to power." "It requires," as Rollo May also says, "the courageous living out of the individual's potentialities in his own particular existence"; " 'will to power' is an ontological category, that is, an inseparable aspect of being." It is the *courage to be* as an individual (in Tillich's sense). Nietzsche's solution needs to be invoked by the new existentialism. As May writes in *Existence—A New Dimension in Psychotherapy:*

Man's task is simple: he should cease letting his "existence" be "a thoughtless accident." Not only the use of the word *Existenz,* but the thought which is at stake, suggests that this essay is particularly close to what is today called *Existenzphilosophie.* Man's fundamental problem is to achieve true "existence" instead of letting his life be no more than just another accident. In *The Gay Science* Nietzsche hits on a formulation which brings out the essential paradox of any distinction between self and true self: "what does your conscience say?—You *shall become who you are*" . . . *Ecco Homo, Wie man wird, was man wird, was man ist.* (p. 31)

The central dynamic and need of life are this expansion, growing, bringing one's inner potentialities into birth in action:

"*Not* for pleasure does man strive," holds Nietzsche, "but for power." . . . "Joy is a *plus-feeling* of power."

This "power" is the power of authentic existence; the values of human life never come about automatically:

Individuality, worth and dignity are not *gegeben* . . . given us as data by nature, but *aufgegeben*—i.e. given or assigned to us as a task which we ourselves must solve. (Ibid.)

May links this with Tillich's view—and with that of Sartre, who insists that "you *are* your choices," with his most positive emphasis.

Kierkegaard, Nietzsche, and Freud each deal, as May emphasizes, with problems of anxiety, despair, and the fragmented personality. What they sought was integration. We are today still seeking for totality. Most of what I have said could be related to Roger Poole's kind of concern to indicate the inadequacies of "objectivity"—and to seek "the totality of problems, objective and subjective, to the *whole* thinker, taking into account all the evidence, both quantifiable and unquantifiable" (*TS*, p. 108).

To adopt an existentialist view is not necessarily to declare that human existence is a nothing, as Heidegger maintained. We must reject the principle of nullity that lurked in the old existentialism. As E. K. Ledermann says, "choosing implies the need to reject the alternative which has not been chosen, and such a rejection is in fact a moral victory for the person." And this victory can be one that is not made futile by death, since the achievement is not nullified by death, but lives on; in this there is the *Dasein* element, the achieved meaning. Nor is this a merely rational achievement; it requires drawing on the depths of our irrationality.

It may seem strange to recommend that education should accept "the realm of the irrational." But it must be made clear what Martin Buber meant by this. He means what psychoanalysis implies: we must, in trying to know ourselves, recognize the darker side of ourselves, the inward life, and the incomprehensible aspects of our life.

On the contrary, the person who knows the world outside or within himself without the use of his ratio gathers far richer knowledge than he can obtain with the aid of the rational principle: "What the most learned and ingenious combination of concepts denies, the humble and faithful beholding, grasping, knowing of any situation bestows. The world is not comprehensible, but it is embraceable: through the embracing of one of its beings." (Buber, quoted in *EN*, p. 72)

"This thing of darkness I acknowledge mine."[14]

Ledermann quotes Buber on the complexity of experience: "each thing and being has a twofold nature: the passive, absorbable, useable, dissectible, comparable, combinable, rationalisable, and the other, the active non-absorbable, undissectible, incomparable, non-combinable, non-rationalisable."

Modern man whose mind has been steeped in rationalism must become aware of the significance of irrationalism which opens the way to that world which is closed to the rational approach. His own personality, and his fellow human beings, the qualities of the inner and outer world, and the significance of the voice of conscience can be grasped only by means of the irrational standpoint. (*EN*, p. 72)

This does not mean a turning away from reality in mystical denial of negation. "By adopting the non-rational attitude, man confronts the world and the people in it, and it discloses its meaning to him."

> The gaining of faith depend upon the ability to face the world irrationally, to hold oneself open to the unconditional mystery which we encounter in every sphere of our life and which cannot be comprised in any formula . . . Real faith means the ability to endure life in the face of this mystery. The forms in which the mystery approaches us are nothing but our personal experiences" . . . By means of the irrational approach, man can gain clarity (although not the clarity of conceptual science), faith in himself and in the world, and freedom from existential neurosis. (*EN,* p. 72, Quotation from Martin Buber, *Israel and the World* [New York: Schocken Books, 1948], p. 49)

In the light of existentialist psychotherapy then, our primary need is to sustain our confidence in the possibility of finding meaning, and the need to discover and exert our authenticity—and our freedom. This requires a more whole embracement of our being, including our deepest bodily life, and the deepest springs of our feelings. There, as so many therapists have found, is no mere brute, but a formative principle and a striving for order and beauty. It is those who cannot become aware of this creative consciousness who become sufferers from a sense of there being no meaning in life, and develop noogenic neuroses.

Everyone is faced with the need to accept his (or her)[15] limitations and to come to terms with them, and if he can accept these *he can still exercise his freedom within the bondage of his restrictions.* His ethical dynamics may not be able to break the bonds of neurotic sickness, but can certainly be exerted against his spiritual deadness. In the face of his being-unto death, he can establish the *Dasein,* the sense of having meaningfully existed.

If he simply refuses to come to terms, or justifies his predicament in some deterministic way, and is persuaded that he cannot break out of his condition, then he may forfeit his freedom as a human being, even though freedom, in the existentialist sense, is the realization of "what he has within himself to become." By refusing responsibility to his creative conscience, man can actually annihilate himself.

But in the work of the (new) existentialist thinkers I have invoked in this book, surely we can begin to see a new way to combat the paralysis of love and will in our time? We can begin to see our way back to creative man who finds his freedom in serving his new best imaginings of future possibilities, and in exercising his moral freedom.

Notes

1. Although Fromm's humanism has its limitations, his *Crisis in Psychoanalysis* (London: Jonathan Cape, 1971) is a book to be read.

2. "Pleasure and Happiness," *Philosophy* 42 (1968): 53.

3. E. K. Ledermann, "The Concept of Man in Psychotherapy," *Proceedings of the Royal Society of Medicine* 47 (1954): 976–77.

4. Frankl postulates a "noölogical dimension" that is not accessible to the beasts, for man can be "capable of reflecting on himself." See *Psychotherapy and Existentialism*, p. 3, and "The Concept of Man in Logotherapy," *Journal of Existentialism* 4 (1965): 53.

5. J. F. T. Bugental, *The Search for Authenticity: An Existential-Analytic Approach to Psychotherapy*, (London: Holt, Rinehard and Winston, 1965).

6. The quotations are from *Ideas: General Introduction to Pure Phenomenology* (London: Allen and Unwin, 1931), pp. 270, 246–47, and 240. See also "The Object," in J. N. Mohanty, "Husserl's Phenomenology," *Philosophy and Phenomenological Research* 14 (1954): 343ff.

7. The word *antepredicative* has caused me more difficulty, in grasping its meaning, than any other word in modern psychology or philosophy. It belongs to the terminology of logic. The predicate is what is predicated, what is affirmed or denied of the subject by means of the copula. To predicate is to assert or affirm predication. An ante-predicative thus means *before it is possible to make such affirmations at all*. It thus refers to all that shadowy, not-yet-conceptual processes in which Michael Polanyi, Marjorie Grene, and Roger Poole are interested: tacit, intuitive processes of apprehension. See also my discussion of Buytendijk and Winnicott on the infant's discovery of reality above.

8. The realities of our dependence may be studied in the films of children suffering separation made by James and Joyce Robertson (Tavistock Institute). And, of course, in John Bowlby's studies of attachment and loss.

9. See my analysis in *Education, Nihilism and Survival*.

10. Karl Stern in *The Flight from Woman* makes the point that "liberated" denial of the difference between man and woman paves the way for further homunculism, and makes it possible for women to be even more exploited. He accuses Simone de Beauvoir particularly of leading to this situation. See also some comments on Mme. de Beauvoir in F. J. J. Buytendijk's *Woman*. Some of the persuasions of militant feminism could have the opposite effect to that which is intended. See Ann Belford Ulanov, *Receiving Woman* (Philadelphia: Westminster Press, 1981), a Jungian view.

11. "Guilt and Guilt Feelings," in *The Knowledge of Man*, ed. Friedman (London: Allen and Unwin, 1964), p. 126.

12. May's quotation of Whitehead is from *Alfred North Whitehead, His Reflections on Man and Nature*, ed. Ruth Narda Ansher (New York: Harper and Row, 1961).

13. See Graham Carey and Peter Abbs, *Design for a New College*, (London: Heinemann Educational Books, 1977).

14. Prospero, about Caliban, in Shakespeare's *The Tempest*.

15. My use of "he" implies no sexist bias; it is simply to make life simpler. The same is true of my use of "man" which means "humankind."

8

Where Shall Wisdom Be Found? And Where Is There a Place for Philosophical Space?

How difficult is the revisionary task that I have outlined for the humanities may perhaps be illuminated by an example. Below I commend Roger Poole for his book *Towards Deep Subjectivity,* in which he urges that we are each allowed the right to a "philosophical space," and one would like to translate that into practice in education. But what hope is there of making such reforms in our institutions? The difficulties may be shown by taking one example from the realm of what is nowadays called "vocationally relevant" education, the world of the polytechnic institute.

Some years ago the present author gave a talk on "creativity" as a visiting speaker at one of Britain's leading colleges of technology, the Manchester College of Science and Technology as it was called then. Of course, the place has changed, its name has changed, and the staff are now all dispersed. But the same problem remains, as one finds all over the world, while in the universities there is an assault on the humanities in general. As visiting lecturer I found that the two thousand students in this institution had no significant time allocated in their timetables to the humanities, and I also found that some of the staff thought that this was wrong. The students had very little time given to the consideration of the question of the aims and purposes of technology, or its history, while no time at all was given to the experience of the subjective disciplines such as imaginative literature or creative writing. In the planning of the syllabus there seemed to be little concern for the personal development of students as persons, and none for the pursuit of the question "What is it to be human?" There was certainly little or no opportunity to ask "What is the point of life?"

The questions that came to mind were: Can any organization that fails to provide such opportunities really be fit to be recognized as an *educational* center? Should it not simply be called a mere vocational training shop? If learning is "a transformation of the whole person," there seemed no provision here for the wholeness of the process, nor for any conscious examination of what was going on, in the world or in the light of values and beliefs. Yet without such force of concern, surely the world is in danger? Who is going to formulate aims unless it is students of such institutions, for they are going to be the people directly concerned with such problems as pollution, misuse of resources, and damage to nature? How can we question what technology is doing effectively unless we train those who operate it to be aware of what is involved in the wider human issues? Overall, there is the question of ends. (See F. R. Leavis, *Education and The University* [London: Chatto and Windus, 1947].)

There followed a correspondence between myself and the then principal of the college, Lord Bowden. It should be made clear that this director of a huge educational establishment was himself aware that all is not well with the world that science and technology are creating. Here, for instance, are some extracts from a speech he made at the Institute of Civil Engineers in 1967:

> Three-quarters of the whole American research and development pro-gramme is now in the defence and space industries. These two enor-mous giants are growing rapidly and inexorably. Whole cities and states depend upon them and would go bankrupt without them. . . . Nearly 80 per cent of the research in M.I.T. is paid for by the Department of Defence. . . . Most of the engineers and scientists in America are sooner or later involved in defence or space. For this reason the whole pattern of education in the United States has been distorted, and it is beginning to appear that the educational system of the world is being distorted, too. . . . The economy of the United States is in an extraordi-nary condition. The real needs of the population, by which I mean their food, their houses, their clothes, their motor cars and so on can be met by the efforts of about half the working population, so the government must find work for the rest. It seems to me that in her defence pro-gramme and space programme America has created the most extrava-gant and sophisticated and most dangerous system of outdoor relief ever devised by a great nation in peacetime. Has there been anything like it since the Government of Imperial Rome ruined itself—and the world around it—by spending 40 per cent of its revenue on the circus.
>
> The riots which have taken place in San Francisco, in Watts County, and in New York, are only the most obvious evidence of the discontent of the submerged part of the American population. It is preposterous that America should try to put a man on the moon when so many thousands of millions of her citizens are living in conditions of squalor devoid even of hope. The forests are being felled, essential ores are being used up, the Great Lakes themselves, the biggest single bodies of fresh water on the face of the earth, are rapidly becoming contaminated, and the St. Lawrence River which drains half the American continent is reported to be unsafe for swimming below Montreal. Millions of citizens who are unable to find work which suits their talents, abilities, and education, view the future with anxiety, and meanwhile this vast Mo-loch is moving slowly onwards, crushing beneath it everything in its way.

This is the view of his world of a leading figure in technological education, responsible for training those who work in these fields. Of science, however, he says:

> We must keep our sense of proportion. We must not forget that science has made our modern world, that it is transforming it before our eyes, that we could not survive without it and its products. We must remember furthermore that modern science is itself one of the supreme achievements of the human intellect. . . . *Science has become too important to be left to scientists.* (Emphasis added)

The latter remarks make an important emphasis, but while such reflections may help us to refrain from blaming science for the way society misuses science, they do not quite reach the problem of how we may *feel* our responsibility and exert it in this sphere, as a question of meaning and "philosophical space." What about leaving technology to technologists? Our responsibility surely needs to be presented to us *even as we learn,* even as we take in the implications of science teaching?

After this, however, Lord Bowden's speech tails off with some remarks about Marxism and about the problem of the "brain drain." He says that "the citizens of a civilized country very properly want to have distinguished scientists among them as much as they want painters and singers and musicians and architects." But Lord Bowden never got down to the question of what the scientist has to undertake, if he is not content merely to serve the Moloch that threatens our whole life and environment. Nor does he say what exactly it is that the painter or musician has to offer. He gives an impression that artists have some kind of "prestige," while the arts generally bedeck our environment. But surely the arts should be— must be—one of the sources of those subjective values by which science and technology can properly serve human ends and not menace them?

It seems to me then that Lord Bowden fell short of an adequate approach to the problem that, one would suppose, was his overall concern. The Moloch is, after all, created by individuals, and the quality of the "life-world" of each determines its nature. The technological developments of which he speaks are created by the human beings working in the enterprises that comprise it. Molochs are created by *us,* and however much it may seem that they become are vast nonhuman Moloch, this Moloch is not impersonal at all, since we are, so to speak, inside it, like Jonah in the whale, except that we are by no means even so helpless, so much apart from it, as such a simile might imply. Just as there is no "impersonal aspect of knowledge" except what arises from "personal participation," so there is no "impersonal Moloch" except that which arises from the "orientation and reorientation" of *"someone"*—or a whole world of someones. Technology is technical workers doing something. We must continually be responsible for the Moloch, for only if we accept responsibility can we change it to a human creature.

The Moloch of which Lord Bowden speaks is created by the individuals whom he was educating, and by the kind of learning they received. So Lord Bowden was perhaps in the best possible position for changing the situation of which he speaks, from the inside. But how much was he aware of the problem that lay behind his speech—the problems of human significance lying behind science and technology? I take Lord Bowden only as a typical representative of the problem we encounter in all higher education: how much awareness is there in the teachers of the relationship between personal culture and technology? F. R. Leavis often criticized the view displayed by leading figures in this sphere: even in the universities they tend to regard culture not as a central discipline, but as a mere source of "graciousness," essentially as a comforting hand of elegance to be added to life: not as "real" as science.

Having read a report of Lord Bowden's speech, I wrote to him as follows:

I was interested to see your remarks, reported in the Press today, that fields elsewhere may remain uncultivated, because America is sending rockets into outer space.

I am myself concerned with "inner space": that is, with creative symbolism in the service of the discovery of human identity, through poetry, and other subjective activities. Here I feel we have problems to solve of finding out who we are, for which we have substituted too much, in our civilisation, the probing of outer space and material preoccupations.

For this reason I was very shocked recently when I attended your Institute of Science and Technology to find that the time-table allowed little or no attention to problems of the inner life. I may be wrong, but I gathered from the lecturers to whom I talked that there seemed to be little "official" recognition of the needs of the students to explore their emotional life, to work on creative problems, to take in the imaginative culture of their civilisation—as part of the syllabus. They don't seem to have provision to discuss the philosophy of science, or subjects such as "the place of science in the modern world." Apart from a few lectures from "outside" people like myself, it seemed that their personality development, their development of the capacities to think and feel in a whole way, and their literacy (in the deepest sense) were left more or less to chance, or to "extra-curricular" activities.

I felt myself that this kind of education itself tends to produce a situation in which a meaningless preoccupation with "outer solutions" arises, since implicit in it is a contempt for subjective reality, as a failure to see that the basis of any science or technology worth having is in the development of whole powers of "being" in those who develop it.

I wonder what your comments would be on this impression of mine?

What caused dismay about the reply that followed my impertinence was the incapacity of Lord Bowden and some of his colleagues even to understand the problem I was trying to raise. Lord Bowden himself replied:

Most of our students are very straightforward extroverted people. We do have our problems, of course, but we have an extremely effective student health centre and both the doctor and some of his nurses provide help, counsel and advice to students who feel that they need it. I hope that you will not feel so worried about us—we are not very worried about ourselves—but it was very kind of you to write.

In his speech Lord Bowden was describing a world—the world of practical empiricism—that seems, by his account, to have lost its sense of direction and proportion—catastrophically. This loss of a sense of direction may be traced to the implicit assumptions about man in his world that are inherent in the kind of learning and aptitude Lord Bowden's college gives, at the expense of other modes. Yet, when I raised the question of how we need to reconsider the assumptions of science and technology, and the nature of learning, he immediately flies to the conclusion that I am talking about "curing" individual "mental illness". He tells me that he and his colleagues "are not worried about themselves"—and yet, from the point of view of his own speech, they ought to be. They may well be serving a vast chimera, a specter of technicism, even while they contentedly pursue their simple-minded "extrovert" preoccupation with manipulating the environment. If they examined the implications and symbolism of it, they might even lose their *raison d'être*, certainly their confidence. But such confidence often seems possible only in those who are blind to the philosophical, moral, and human problems of their own "practical" subjects and to the basic problems of technology in the world, even the kind Lord Bowden had touched on in his speech.

The reactions of Lord Bowden's staff were more revealing. The head of one department wrote that in talking to me he got the impression that I "considered everyone who is being educated, whether schoolchild or university graduate, as a subject for psychiatric investigation."

[Holbrook's] view is that all students are in some measure maladjusted and in need of remedial treatment and that all courses should therefore be adapted for this purpose. My own view is that most students are healthy extroverts who know they have a job to do and are keen to get on with it.

Such antagonism to a concern with human meaning seems to be the penalty for raising the problem of existence and the nature of knowledge *at all.* The hostility seems to reveal in unquestioned attachment to that "bustle" which Buber believes distracts us comfortably from confronting the problem of existence. "Healthy extroverts" subscribe to the developments guided by "objectivity"—and simply get on with a job. They do not reflect. But that is just the trouble, as the acid rain falls and the lakes are poisoned, nuclear reactors explode and cities breed alienation.

Thus "healthy extroverts" are creating a world in which millions of citizens are faced with anxiety, frustration, and failure to use their potential talents. They are creating that world which Rollo May diagnoses as schizoid. They are even destroying the physical resources of the earth. This is bad enough. But to raise the problems of existential significance behind technology and the education that serves it is to imply, apparently, that everyone should be the subject of "psychiatric investigation." Yet, as Viktor Frankl points out, to suffer from existential frustration and a sense of meaninglessness is by no means "sick"; it may arise from an intelligent concern with meaning and values.

The staff member whom I quoted seems unwilling to have the assumptions of "extrovert" devotion to "making things go" examined in themselves, and related to the needs of human beings and the quality of civilization. He seems to me to show a characteristic unwillingness to submit science and technology themselves as human disciplines to philosophical examination. Despite their assumed "objectivity" many such disciplines have subjective roots—as, for instance, in the impelling confidence in "progress." There may even be in them a manic quality, as on the denial of death and human dependency. In this there may be a rejection of profound moral issues. I think, for example, of countries in which the lives of many people are primitive and poor, yet these countries feel they must display an advanced air transport system to the world.

In such ways, the preoccupation with outward functions seems to be, sometimes, an avoidance of the complexity and intractability of human problems that reveal themselves, in the end, to be subjective ones—requiring, perhaps, forms of cooperation, justice, and fairness that can be achieved only if "subjective" problems of prejudice, human equality, or the sharing of power are dealt with. I am thinking of schemes requiring cooperation on a local plane, for irrigation or the improvement of agriculture. In our own world, manifestations such as the space race, "defense," and even the development of fast air travel, seem to represent the distorted use of resources when one considers the plight of many poor countries in the world. Our resources are devoted, for example, to an intensely electronic and industrialized culture that seems to be of doubtful educational value, and to an as intensely electronic domestic life (with ovens worked by computers and so on)—and these may only be seeming to make our life better in quality, or seeming only to make order out of chaos. To some, they seem to be the last manifestations, like space rockets, of the male proclivity for manipulating the world.

Erikson says, "they perhaps show now the limits of this kind of imaginative effort." To be an "extrovert," following these blindly without being aware of their subjective meaning, may itself be something very far from "healthy," and may be extremely unreasonable and even criminal. Technology, far from being a form of "progress," may (like the reckless use of fossil fuels) be jeopardizing man's survival. It is often as if, in the words of a psychoanalyst writing on the specters of technicism: "the spirit of meeting specifications in . . . human ventures had taken flight from responsible human agents and become an independent reality—a reality which has come to overhang the modern world and to enter into the dynamic processes of personality—as a spectral object" (Robert W. Daly). Lord Bowden himself seems concerned (in his speech) about many of these false paths, but charity surely begins at home?

From the reply of the member of the Manchester staff, it seemed that the only courses in the humanities proper in this college consisted of "combined studies courses where the history and institutions of a particular country and its people are studied," and course in the history of science. The lecturer angrily concludes:

> I would remind Mr. Holbrook that this is a faculty of Technology in a University not a psychiatric department in a mental home. It is a great mistake to assume because some undergraduates need to have recourse to the psychiatrist that this is a norm and also erroneous to believe that a student of this institution who is interested in his academic discipline does not find in it the stimulus and interest to give him satisfaction.
> Mr. Holbrook is mainly interested in the therapeutic effects of self-expression, particularly of poetry writing, on people who are confused and depressed by their studies. I feel that his remarks are not relevant to the situation as it exists in this Faculty.

My concern was never to restore "mental health" to those who are "depressed by their studies," though plenty of students have cause enough to be so depressed. My concern was to foster the exploration of the *nature and meaning of being human,* at a time when the confidence we are asked to sustain in technicism and other ways of manipulating the world has suffered a number of severe blows and can no longer be endorsed with whole-hearted assurance.

Lord Bowden shows himself disturbed by the way some developments in the world have been going. Is he then "maladjusted"? Of course not. He even shows in his speech a gleam of existential doubt. But from my point of view he is certainly not depressed enough, and I find it difficult to see how he can reccncile the confidence of his letters to me with the doubts of his speech, except to suppose that he does not really want the dynamics of technology questioned.

Another lecturer from the Department of Management Sciences at Manchester was less inclined to resist my approach. Of course, such a lecturer is correct in pointing to the satisfactions that science and technical skills can give. Of course, many find a sense of meaning in such work. No one wants a retreat from science or a reduction of technological skills. But the satisfactions that science and technology can give are limited to a particular dimension, a concern with what is "out there" in the realm of masculine thinking and doing. Despite their subjective elements, they cannot give an account of *inner space* nor create any new structures or meanings there. They cannot in themselves supply us with an account of man that can guide the *directions* of technological efforts, nor can they create new values toward which we can aspire. This lecturer shows himself somewhat confused about these distinctions:

> When he uses phrases like "inner life," "creative problems," "finding out who we are," it seems to me that these should be used within a subject, rather than as an outside extra. In the sense in which he uses the phrase, a man's "inner life" should be his relationship to his craft. This is discovered surely, by the way in which he studies, not by adding some extra course labelled "philosophy of Science." I would have thought there was a lot to be said for blurring the distinction between the arts and the sciences. The chemical experiment is as much concerned with "inner space" as poetry. I am also suspicious of a world like "wholeness." Surely this word too easily equals the famous English "dilettantism." Naturally I am very concerned that people should have some breadth of vision, but it seems to me all too easy to get lost in these spatial analogies. In the end it is character, not knowledge, which is the decisive factor. A good engineer is just as creative and "whole" as a "good" artist. Surely, too, the barbarians are such whatever their subject. People who were pointed out to us as heroes in the Cambridge in which I was brought up were those who devoted their lives to studying one Greek particle. I still find such whole hearted specialisation admirable: but that has nothing to do with whether I think a particular individual is making the most of life.

This individual does see that more personal contact might supply a source of humanness.

> I would have thought if it was possible at all to programme the sort of things for which Holbrook is asking into a syllabus, it was through the individual contact between the teacher and the student.

But he fails to see that culture is concerned with the pursuit of human meaning and significance, which it cannot be the task of science and technology to give, and that this is a *philosophical* task. Yet, as we have seen, there are serious human problems lurking behind the assumptions of science itself, while technology cannot itself answer the question "What for?" Inner space has to do with the subjective life, and chemistry is *not* about "inner space" in my sense, the area of moral being, dynamics of life in us that are often outraged by a science that has failed to find man's moral being or his inner needs, as in experimentation with animals, bioengineering, and the manufacture of chemical weapons. If science has stripped the world of meaning, then we need to invoke the other "half of knowledge" to try to restore it.

There is also the problem of establishing an adequate *account of man,* which science cannot give, and which technology is not concerned with. This is a larger problem than discussing with students how "the meaning of life" "ties up with their daily work." It is something more profound than anything that is likely to be discussed in Management Training Courses, Apprenticeship Courses, and Induction Courses. And it cannot be left to "informality." The lecturer continues:

> Since I have been here, I have been talking to some students about the society we had when I was at Cambridge, called "poets' pub." This was an informal group of staff and students to stimulate just the sort of activities which Holbrook would wish. But it was essentially informal.

The underlying attitude here is that what I was proposing is in itself a pastime, recreational, a thing for the "pub,"—a philistine attitude to the arts, of course, that has been predominant in our society since the seventeenth century, or since Galileo, whose distrust of the Poetic was so profound. This attitude also goes with the belief that, if the concern with human ends is to be introduced, it should perhaps by through "discussion" about, rather than the experience of exploring one's own human qualities, and developing one's own potential. The lecturer adds:

> It would seem to me that there might possibly be scope for some sort of pilot experiment in the developing of informal discussion groups for getting people to *think more widely about their place in society.* (Emphasis added)

The way the lecturer puts the problem as he sees it seems to imply that there would be an answer in terms of *explicit* knowledge, and at most some kind of sociology. Students should perhaps be brought to see how they can "adjust" to "society" (or not, as the case may be). But something much more is needed, and that is a way of knowledge that alters the whole person in a much more radical way, something more *committed,* that belongs to emotion and being—belongs, in fact, to the "other" way of knowing, in an experience of meaning, and that will be likely to foster an "intentionality" that may demand profound changes in society.[1] It may offer a profound critique of society in its concern for human creativity, fulfillment, and meaning, such as we find in, say, Wordsworth, Matthew Arnold, Mrs. Gaskell, T. S. Eliot, and Lawrence himself. There can be a human and creative spirit in industry, too, of course, as we know from the life and work of Isabard Kingdom Brunel, and from Dickens's Daniel Doyce. Some of our greatest scientists and technologists have been aware of the deepest needs of humanity, and some have been in the forefront of movements to do with values and freedom. So, in the humanities, we must continue to insist that human needs come first.

Such "pilot experiments" no doubt would be a step. But I was seeking something more. One knows very well from experience that "discussions" can easily become a kind of exchange that never moves, beyond an exchange of cliché and stereotyped responses, remaining at a superficial explicit level, unless challenges are introduced by a highly skilled leader in a situation in which energies are released by individual creativity or as a genuine contact is made with culture. Knowledge must *change* individuals as Coleridge's term "growledge" implies it should do and is the path to freedom through such change. What we need is an *ontological* discipline. Creative experience is one effective way to such inner change, at the tacit level. But such a discussion can also be prompted and controlled by an imaginative text or work from a distinguished mind, which presents the problems of identity and the meaning of existence in some "felt" human way. It could be a piece of music, drama, or painting, or, indeed, a passage from biology or the philosophy of science. But the best focus might well be a novel like, say, *The Rainbow,* or a Shakespeare play or even a Greek tragedy. So while this lecturer is making some concession to my demand, it is clear that he does not really see the problem, which is a problem that has to do with the primary human needs of symbolism and the sense of *meaning:* subjective disciplines. He sees the problem only as industry and commerce tend to see the use of creative potentialities: they are resources to be exploited.

> Just as the industrial sociologists are saying that the conscious placing of innovators in an organisation is the only way to overcome stagnation, so the conscious placement of *ideas men* might be desirable in a place like this.

It was not "ideas" in this sense that I meant; nor can "ideas" provide the experience we need, except by raising the question of meaning and significance in the realm of thought itself. In any case, the way in which the phrase *ideas men* is used in itself limited here. It belongs to industrial planning and advertizing, in which "ideas" men produce "angles" or "gimmicks" that can subserve commerce and industry. "Ideas" in this sense means solutions to utilitarian, immediate problems. In such a point of view intellect is confined in such a way as to inhibit it from offering any radical challenge to the whole reality of the existing set-up, in terms of ideas (such as we may draw from Ancient Greece) about the quality of life.

All the replies from Manchester were rather in terms of a riposte that mine was "a questionable attitude towards the subject at all. . . ." This was the view of Lord Bowden's member of staff, who continued: "There is a very vigorous student life about this place and . . . we do not see much evidence that the emotional life is atrophied." Yet, surely, emotional atrophy and the "ebbing of humanness" are everywhere visible, in the world created by the products of technical colleges. Many of the problems of our world arise because it is created by people who remain unaware that there are any problems of significance—or even of *understanding*—lurking behind their work.[2] What the products of our technical training institutes *make* and *do* often menaces us; if they were educated as fully aware men and women they might help us become more human. The underlying assumptions in Manchester, when examined closely, are revealed as those of pragmatic utilitarianism, so that "practical applications" are to be taken as ends in themselves and beyond criticism. The existential problems of the relationship between the individual and his whole world, his need for a sense of meaning in life, his problems of being and identity, are felt by such educational centers to be so irrelevant as to be relegated to out-of-school hours, to "personality"—even in a technological world that towers above us, crushing the person. *But this is exactly what is wrong with our society* as Rollo May makes plain.

At the same time these centers seem to cling to the view that the learning *they* impart is not "personal," but belongs to some impersonal entity. Because science and technology are effective, they must be served like gods and the inevitable problem of what is assumed in exercising them is forgotten. This is a version of the "false goal of objectivity." For even scientific learning involves (if Polanyi is right) changes in persons, inevitably; it is rooted in men's doing something. In the absence of recognition of this, and responsibility to it, the problems that arise, the effect is likely to be dehumanization. The very determination of such teachers to exclude any recognition or any questioning of the meaning and implications of their work is itself dehumanizing. The whole problem of which Lord Bowden himself spoke is a problem created by such implicit depersonalization, such submission of the individual to an assumed body of "objective" knowledge of a pragmatic purpose that is taken to be larger than him, greater in itself than all individual human aims, so that his life must inevitably subserve it. People trained in such ways are likely to be so split that in their manipulation of the environment they become dissociated from their own humanness. Existentialism would suggest that we need to recover our humanness and so need to reconsider in a radical way the nature of what we are doing, and look at the human implications. The Manchester lecturers seemed strangely unwilling to open up these questions to Socratic dialogue.

My final reply to Lord Bowden and his colleagues was thus:

Your students are the people who will have to make decisions involving human life and its conditions on earth—they are the people who have to decide whether to drown Upper Teesdale, or launch Torrey Canyons, [a reference to a huge oil tanker disaster] or poison the natural life here, or to grow three blades of wheat there, where only one grew before, or develop methods of birth control, or build gasometers in Abingdon. What such people need, urgently, is a developed personal "ethical system." This can only be developed through the imaginative exploration of the subjective world, by which insight and sympathy is gained. Symbolism, according to Susanne Langer, is a primary need of man: she means essentially that poetic symbolism by which individuals solve their problems of identity. And on a deep sense of the potentialities of the human being only can a better world be built. . . .

It is not "therapy" to provide for these in an educational syllabus. It is to concern oneself to ensure that the products of any educational setup shall produce civilised individuals, as whole as they can be, so that the technological world, instead of becoming increasingly philistine and dehumanized, shall learn to make better use of its mechanical and scientific powers.

Don't you think students of science and technology ought to be impelled more by a sense of human values—something more than just a sense of having "a job to do"? One look at the ugliness and inefficiency, and the ugly and inhuman environment, often created by science and technology, in America, and over here, too, makes one very doubtful surely of your assertion that you "are not worried about yourselves." You ought to be!

In his original Proposals for the Development of Manchester College of Science and Technology, Lord Bowden ends his enthusiastic general introduction by saying "we must have technology for the sake of survival." Yet in his address quoted above he seems to imply that our survival itself is threatened by technology. What then? But in their uses, do science and technology foster—or threaten—survival? Not only does an education that is deficient in attention to the "other" way of knowing produce students less well able to question human aims and values, and to be critical of the assumptions behind their work, but it actually makes them less effective as scientists and technicians, because it confines their capacities to perceive what there is "there" to be dealt with in the world. Where science and technology fail to make the best use of human resources, they are being *inefficient,* because of a failure of human meaning.

Education can transform society by making human beings conscious of their potentialities as creatures, so that in time they will demand a society in which they can be free to realize themselves. But such realization cannot simply arise from the material surroundings, comfort, or acquisition. It is a question of helping human beings to find answers to the question "What is it to be human?" and "What is the point of life?" in the light of the wind of either-or alternative implied by my quotation above about Kierkegaard.

Lord Bowden quotes Bertrand Russell earlier in his introduction:

We may smile at our ancestors, but only twenty years ago Bertrand Russell attributed the bitterness and cynicism of many university students to their "consciousness that their work had no real importance," and an Oxford don found that "many thoughtful undergraduates are growing weary of pursuing half heartedly a course of study that they know to be none too good, and vaguely attempting to supplement it with occasional gems picked up from sideshows."

But doesn't Lord Bowden's account of the predicament of science and technology in America imply that much of the work of these individuals in human terms has "no real importance," while science and technology themselves may not have found their sense of proportion? From the account given by one of Lord Bowden's lecturers alone, of the courses run at Manchester as being "concerned to make a person a walking encyclopedia," may it not still be true that students there may be "weary" of "not too good" courses? Certainly, from the point of view of the lecturers whose replies are discussed above, any gems from the humanities seem to be regarded as "only to be picked up from the side shows."

None of this is to be taken to imply that we need not educate for industry, or even that industry is in some way to be despised. There is now even a committee in Britain to promote attention to and admiration for industry: the slogan is "Thanks to industry." And it is true in a sense that culture and the humanities depend upon industrial success to produce their funds. But it is also true that technology, industry, science, and commerce are only instruments to serve human ends. In my terms these are ends of *being.* The consideration of the proper ends has fallen a long way behind the progress of development of the tools; that is why a new spirit and impetus need to be given to the humanities.

Notes

1. Something, one might even say, more tragic, devoted to ultimate meanings in the face of death, and the *Dasein* need.

2. To say nothing of the actual physical nature of some of the environments on university campuses—brutal and mean architecture, ugly spaces, endless noise within and without, functional services, and a lack of the numinous—a gracelessness in which one would blush to speak of beauty.

Conclusions

Our conclusions must be that the process of realigning our view of man in the light of the philosophical tradition I have been invoking has hardly begun, and we have a prodigious task ahead of us. The task is nothing less than rejecting the established view of the mind, which is passive and sensation-bound in the Humean legacy, and substituting that (Liebnitzian) more positive view which is to be found in Continental philosophy and in the native work of Samuel Taylor Coleridge.

One recent work should be mentioned: *Towards Deep Subjectivity* by Roger Poole, a lecturer in English at the University of Nottingham, which contributes to the debate by insisting on each man's right to pursue his own philosophical investigation. The phrase that links Poole with Marjorie Grene is Husserl's "a shaft of attention"; we do not merely passively receive "impressions" or "stimuli" from the world. We *see* it, in a positive sense. We see with intentionality, and we throw out of ourselves a developed shaft of sensing attention that terminates in the object. We make the world as we see it (and we were taught to do this by our mothers). There is no "objective" world, to all intents and purposes, to which we must submit ourselves because of its daunting "truth." Of course, this is not to say that it wouldn't exist if all human beings died, it is really "there" all right. But it would not be *known;* and the whole essence of our problem is how and what we know—consciousness itself. "The world . . . is not the spatial support of mathematically known extension, but a world of interacting subjectivities which belong to people, which they confer meaning upon and *control* through their conferring meaning upon it" (*TS*, p. 88).

This explains why, as Poole makes plain, quoting Husserl, "no objective science, no matter how exact, explains or can explain anything in a serious sense."

Once we accept these insights into the limitations of "objectivity," we can no longer separate the thinker from the thought, or "objective science" from its responsibilities, or "man" from "fact." The absurdities and evils that "objectivity" has caused must no longer be tolerated. The truth of our observation of the world is more complex. "The objects in the world are seen from different perspectives. We move around them, seeing them and experiencing them in different modalities, while other people in

150

the world do the same. We are all conscious that there is only one world, but we are also quite sure that we all see it differently, and we all attribute different meanings to it at various times. The world is a communalized set of perspectives. Nothing is ever fixed, everything is subject to the meaning we give it. Thus in general the world exists not only for isolated men but for the community of man" (*TS*, pp. 89–90).

The upshot of the new perspective to which Poole is trying to draw our attention is that, if we accept it, it places upon us a profound ethical responsibility—to the world, to man in the world, and to *man's knowing himself*. The responsibility to knowing means that, since the world is "a world of interacting subjectivities," we need to reintegrate subjective research and to find a more adequate "objectivity" that *contains* the realm of subjectivity. "The consistent way I operate my intentionality the consistent way, that is, that I confer meaning according to certain shapes and necessities (which after a while become predictable), offers the interpreter of the subjective world his first vital clue. With this attention to the 'intentionality' of subjects in the world (the way they confer meaning and interpret their world) the massive task of reintegrating subjectivity into objective research has begun" (*TS*, p. 92).

Here we meet the problem stated by Marjorie Grene: "only when a deep-lying conceptual reform in our view of knowledge has been assimilated, when we have overcome within ourselves our Cartesian fear of the category of life, and our Newtonian simple-minded-ness about the nature of the nature we strive to know, only then will we be able to open our minds to a new and richer ontology. Such an ontology, to be adequate to the facts of our cognitive experience, will have to include the recognition of the multiplicity of forms as an aspect of the multidimensionality of being (see Edward Pols, *The Recognition of Reason,* 1963)" (*KK*, p. 224).

So, our task in the Humanities is to insist that we have a right to philosophize, and not to leave this to the specialists. Analysis has to be done, not in terms that *exclude* as much as possible (the traditional philosophical-positivist belief) but in terms that *include as much as possible*—and this needs a new set of conceptual instruments. At the end of his book Poole discusses "philosophical space," the embodied position of philosophy as a human activity in the world. He rejects the idea that philosophy is an activity for professionals in universities "like strategy is something done by strategists in the Pentagon or Kremlin." We have been browbeaten into passively accepting philosophies as something handed down to us.

In truth, "every one of us has a right to a philosophy of his own, a right to a space he can think in, a right to his subjective thought-world" (*TS*, p. 142). This assertion of a personal philosophical space goes with an assertion of the need for a new ethical dynamic of commitment. Instead of being "numbed into silence and inanition" we need to have "visible alternatives of action" offered us, together with opportunities to explore appropriate criteria by which to justify such action. We require each to exert his personally won space to think in, "a voice in the conduct of affairs," and "to participate in the way things are directed."

The word *subjectivity*, of course, has become a pejorative word. But Poole has no impulse to encourage an introvert withdrawal from the world. He hopes to generate a new and more adequate "whole" objectivity. At the same time he extends "philosophy" to mean a way of seeking authentic living in the existentialist sense. The development of a more adequate "philosophical space" at large is put before us as a form of suffering, urgent and exacting. Moreover, the subjective disciplines at our disposal are not easy to define or adopt; we are to restore

> personal commitment, ethical concern, desire to treat of the totality, necessity of taking account of the reality or perspectival variation and distortion, necessity at taking account of variations of operative criteria, the use of strange or unquantifiable collocations of evidence of information (such as sheaves and profiles), comparison, inter-relation, description, as well as sympathy, empathy, and antipathy. These tools are no doubt a strange lot, but in my view they have a chance of dealing with complex problems in a way that objective tools do not. (*TS*, p. 125)

For "established" philosophy, no doubt, they do seem an odd collection. But, if Marjorie Grene is right, philosophy has for too long deceived itself in supposing an account of the world could be given adequately by other methods.

There is nothing anti-scientific or anti-objective about Poole's book. It is simply asking for a more adequate approach to truth. "Deep subjectivity emerges finally then as a concern for objectivity, for a full, real and adequate objectivity in order to express this concern it has to discover (first of all) and then trust to (even harder) a space of personally won philosophical commitment" (*TS*, p. 152).

Poole draws our attention to Edmund Husserl, who writes in his introduction to *Ideas:*

> I experience myself here in the first instance as an "I" in the ordinary sense of the term, as this human person living among others in the world. As a psychologist I take as my theme this I-type of being and life, in its general aspect, the human being as "psychical." Turning always in pure reflection, following exclusively "inner experience" and "empathy" to be more precise, and setting aside all the psycho-physical questions which relate to man as corporeal being, I obtain an original and pure descriptive knowledge of the psychical life as it is in itself, the most original information being obtained from myself, because here alone perception is the medium. (*Ideas*, p. 7)

There may be a great deal to criticize in Husserl's phenomenology, and Poole himself admits that, philosophically speaking, Husserl's work ended in failure. But in his best work, as in this passage, Husserl raised important questions of the humanities—as indeed, does all "philosophical anthropology," which attempts to give an account of human nature through the subjective disciplines. How do we know about man? Husserl's answer is, evidently, by knowing myself, my "inner world." And, of course, one's own subjective life is inevitably and inextricably known through intersubjectivity. Education is all about intersubjectivity; even if it were only (as it is not) the taking in of information, this could not be achieved except by processes largely subjective.

The Cartesian-Newtonian world was, says Marjorie Grene, a world without life. This simple fact had and still has disastrous consequences for our ideas of what "knowledge" is and what "knowing" is; what a *knower* is. "These consequences lie so deep in our habits of thought that the recovery from them is slow and difficult" (*KK,* p. 14). It is this prospect of a slow and difficult emergence that daunts one from the outset. The way is littered with failures, like Husserl's failure to complete a phenomenology. Yet, as he said, *this is the inevitable plight* of those who are "educated by the genuine philosophers of the past," "to live for truth." The "history of philosophy, seen from within, takes on the character of a struggle for existence, i.e., a struggle between the philosophy which lives in the straightforward pursuit of its task . . . and the scepticism which negates or repudiates it in empiricist fashion" (*The Crisis of the European Sciences,* p. 13). In this struggle Husserl can only offer us work, too. Philosophers, he declares, have fallen into a painful existential contradiction. The faith in the possibility of philosophy as a task, that is, in the possibility of universal knowledge, is something they *cannot let go:* "We *know* that we are *called* to this task as serious philosophers." And yet how do they hold on to this goal? He believes that in their philosophizing philosophers should be *"functionaries of mankind"*—concerned toward a *telos* and pursuing something that can only come to realization, "if at all," through philosophy.

Is there, in this existential "if," a way out? If not, what should we, who *believe,* do in order to *be able* to believe? (Husserl, *Crisis,* p. 17)

One does not have to go far to find philosophers, even in education, who do not see that philosophy, or indeed any other humanities discipline, should be directed toward finding some way in which *we may be able to believe.* But, unless we are to collapse into nihilism, unless our whole symbolic system is to collapse, it is this at which we must work—something to believe in. At least one may be encouraged by one's students. They want something to believe in, and they are delighted to find an adult who is willing, like Husserl, to "speak according to his best lights" and "live in all seriousness the fate of a philosophical existent" (ibid., p. 18). It is true that, as Spiegelberg says, "not only did Husserl fail to give a complete outline of his phenomenological psychology, but one finds surprisingly few concrete traces of his specific psychological insights in the subsequent literature." But his was not a total failure. For, he goes on, "it was not Husserl the phenomenological *psychologist,* who proved to be the major contributor to the development of psychology. It was the *philosopher* Husserl whose general conception of phenomenology as the science of intentional consciousness, to be described in its essential structures, provided the major impulse for the future" (ibid., p. 13).[1]

Husserl declared that if we strike through the crust of the "historical facts" of philosophical history, "interrogating, exhibiting, and testing their inner meaning and hidden telology,"

> gradually, at first unnoticed but growing more and more pressing, possibilities for a complete reorientation of view will make themselves felt, pointing to new dimensions. Questions, never before asked, will arise; fields of endeavour, never before grasped or radically understood, will show themselves. (*Crisis,* p. 18)

Philosophy will be transformed, and it will be seen that the philosophy of the past (unbeknown to itself) was inwardly oriented toward this new sense of philosophy.

I have hardly taken up my pen, but I must end. Yet I have only touched the edge of the huge revolution indicated by philosophical anthropology, and it is not really my task to interpret it. It is up to the philosophers to pursue the subject. A proper conclusion would pursue the issues raised in Marjorie Grene's final chapter of *The Knower and the Known,* "Time and Teleology."

In Heidegger's philosophy, time merely moves toward the cessation of life. This is the time of all nihilistic philosophies, in which we snatch whatever we can out of our movement toward nothingness, and yet nothing can ever be snatched that is not absurd. We may link this with the Cartesian atomicity of time; if our exploration of the world is chopped up into fragmentary bits of sensation in time, then our existence looks futile, because man disappears.

Polanyi's unit of tacit knowing makes the nature of knowledge, of conscious and aware existence, totally different. In this view we are reaching out from ourselves to the world, and reaching out from past to future. Knowing is a temporal activity, drawn by the future pull of what we seek to understand. Using such concepts, Marjorie Grene argues that learning is a telic phenomenon—a moving toward achievement, which is a pervasive character of life. Living things depend on the future as primary. Time, as lived time, is telic in structure.

In the light of this new existentialist view, "What spreads out before us here in the variety of life's achievements is not so much Heidegger's 'being to death' as Tillich's openness to the future." "Protensions are temporal arches, curved times reaching back from their goals to the steps that lead to them" (*The Knower and the Known* p. 245). Of course, the time measured by physics exists. But our time is *lived* time; in our time "Something not yet born is striving towards a being that pulls it forward to maturity."

Our life is in a time that is a multiplicity of protensions, and is neither time in the Cartesian way nor a smoothly flowing continuum like Newton's true mathematical time. And as with time, so with space. Matter, in the existentialist view, is not over against us in the way of "shoving its meanings down on us." Our experience becomes what Marjorie Grene calls "the protensive pull of our transcendence that is the core of conscious life," and what we transcend is the material of our "being in the world." While we must accept our "condition" and our historical situation,

> in every act of every responsible person the totality of the past is brought to bear, is focussed on the discovery of a meaning still to be known. . . . freedom lives in the openness to the future that is the meaning of the past. (*KK*, p. 252)

Pain, she says, is terrible because it robs us of potentiality, makes life wholly present and therefore meaningless. Afflictions such as confinement, deprivation, and torture are also terrible because they "strangle freedom." Freedom lies in our openness to the future, and we can lose it. Something of the same happens to us, as Maslow and others argue in *Towards a Philosophy of Being*, when we become trapped in an attachment to the material, the concrete, and the present, in our attitude to the world, our philosophy of life.

So the word *intentionality* is a key term in philosophical anthropology, and raises important questions of being and time. It is a concept from Husserl and is declared by Rollo May to be "the structure which gives meaning to experience." May returns again and again to the question of intentionality in his books such as *Love and Will* and *Existence—A New Dimension in Psychiatry*, the latter of which provides us with a historical survey of the developments of existential thought especially in its relevance to psychotherapy. Intentionality, May says, is not to be identified with intentions, but is the dimension that underlies them: "It is our imaginative participation in the coming day's possibilities" (*Love and Will*, p. 224).[2] Our intentions are decisive, he says, with respect to how we perceive the world. "But this is only one side of intentionality. The other side is that it also does come from the object. Intentionality is the bridge between these. It is the structure of meaning that makes it possible for us, subjects that we are, to see and understand the outside world, objective as it is. In intentionality, the dichotomy between subject and object is partially overcome" (*LW*, p. 225).

Intentionality may be the clue to the problem of subject and object. Yet, as May says, it is a concept that seems "important and has been . . . neglected in contemporary psychology." May traces the concept historically back to Aristotle and St. Thomas Aquinas, and finds it an early epistemology concerned with how we know reality. St. Thomas said: "The intellect through a species of being informed in the art of intelligence, forms itself some intention of the understood thing." Husserl extended the concept to the whole of our knowledge. consciousness, he pointed out, never exists in a subjective vacuum but is always *consciousness of something*. "Meaning is an intention of the mind," in Husserl's words. "The art and experience of consciousness itself is a continuous moulding and remoulding of our world, self related to objects and objects to self in inseparable ways, self participating in the world as well as observing it, neither pole of the self or world being conceivable without the other" (p. 227). It has to do with knowing as a mode of being-in-the-world. The teacher working with a child or student who is working on his experience through creative modes including symbolism is only too aware of this: that seeing and learning are processes of whole growth.

The experimental psychologist separates the poles of subjectivity and objectivity. Of course, there is no objection to this for certain purposes. Rollo May explains: "This, of course, does not mean that we cannot bracket for the moment the subjective or objective side of the experience. When I measure my house to see how much paint it will take to repaint it, or when I get a report on some endocrinological tests on my children, I bracket for the moment how I feel about it: I want only to understand as clearly as I can these measurements. But *then* my responsibility is to put these objective facts back into the context in which they have meaning for me—my project to paint my house, or my caring for the health of my child. I *believe that one of our serious errors in psychology is to bracket out part of experience and never put it back together again*" (*LW*, p. 27, emphasis added). Disaster arises only when psychologists fall so much under the spell of the divorce that they can no longer put together and see as whole what it is they have put asunder.

The revolution in thought that we are trying to grasp may be traced to what May calls Immanuel Kant's "second Copernican revolution." Kant held that the mind is not simply passive clay on which sensations write, nor something that merely absorbs and classifies facts. What really happens is that objects themselves conform to our ways of understanding" (*LW*, p. 226). "Kant's revolution lay," says May, "in making the human mind an active, forming participant in what it knows. Understanding itself is then *constitutive of the world.*" What we are groping toward is that state for which Roger Poole seeks—"a point of vantage from where we point out that we are *conferring meaning on the world,* instead of letting the world shove its meanings down on us."[3] We are concerned here to involve the Continental view of the mind, which finds it an active constituent of reality (Liebnitz) rather than a passive one (Locke).

Husserl was a disciple of Franz Brentano (whose lectures in the University of Vienna were also attended by Freud). "The concept of intentionality was reintroduced (in the nineteenth century) by Franz Brentano . . . [who] believed that consciousness is defined by the fact that it *intends* something, points towards something outside itself—specifically, that it *intends the object.* Thus, intentionality gives meaningful contents to consciousness" (*LW*, p. 226).

Roger Poole declares that intentionality is the "central thought-dimension which differentiates all phenomenological thinking. . . . the concept of intentionality . . . assumes the creative presence of human freedom in perception and thought. Intentionality, crudely spelled out, is the presence of freedom in meaning-conferring in the perceiving subject. The subject as observed by the phenomenologist confers meaning upon the world, and, in doing so, implicitly asserts his freedom . . ." (*Universities Quarterly* [1974], p. 498).

In this approach to philosophy the mind is back in the body and person: "there can never be anything other than persons knowing," but also "there is no experience except as shaped by the mind's activity" (*KK*, p. 142). "The knowing mind is always the whole person" (*KK*, p. 57). Moreover, we need to recognize the positive role of consciousness in our perception of the world. Marjorie Grene refers us to Polanyi's approach, "illustrating the existentialist thesis that our being is *being in a world.* . . . My awareness is not a separate subjective 'in-itself,' but at one and the same time an assimilation of what is beyond and an extension of myself into the things beyond. This interpretation of 'self' and 'world' is not only a central characteristic of mind: it is what mind is" (*KK*, p. 56).

If we see our relationship between "self" and "world" in this complex way of interacting, in dwelling, between perception and appreciation (a complexity fully endorsed by the findings of both psychoanalysts and biologists who have explored encounter), and its relationship of perception and action of the "being-in-the-world," then we may find our way toward a more adequate way of exploring our existence—by attention to the *Lebenswelt,* the complex of whole being, involving subjective and objective. This should restore, too, such dynamics as intentionality.

In Grene's words, "we *are* the upsurge of time, and the present and even the vision of the past and of futurity, out of its projection of what we long to be—creative imagination, through which we shape the time that we are: this is our most essential gift . . ." (*KK*, p. 143).

Abraham Maslow argues that in philosophical anthropology there is not only a body of human truth from which a humanistic system of values can be created, but also a recognition of ultimate principles in human life:

> It looks as if *there were* a single ultimate value for all mankind, a far goal towards which all men strive. This is called variously by different authors: self-actualization, self-realization, integration, psychological health, individuation, autonomy, creativity, productivity . . . but they all agree that this amounts to realizing the potentialities of the person, that is to say, becoming fully human, everything that the person *can* become. (*New Knowledge in Human Values*, p. 123)

Becoming, he emphasizes, leads to Being, in those experiences of peak moments at which we feel that we have established a meaning in our lives. These experiences of order and meaning are the source of values. Even so, to point to such knowledge is not to say that it is easily available in the final form necessary on which to base conviction or action. But the keynote is one of optimism:

> What *is* available, however, is enough to give us confidence that we know the kinds of work that have to be done in order to progress towards such a goal. It appears possible for man, by his own philosophical and scientific efforts, to move towards self-improvement and social improvement. (Ibid., p. viii)

Maslow's book opens by recognizing our disease as "the lack of something to believe in" (p. vii). In the symposium Ludwig Von Bertalanffy, director of biological research at Mount Sinai Hospital at the University of California, says that "a new symbolic universe of values must be saved from the pit of meaninglessness, suicide and atomic fire." Humanists, says Maslow, have for years been trying to construct a naturalistic, psychological value system derived from man's own nature. Today it is possible for the first time to feel confident that this age-old hope may be fulfilled, *if we strive hard enough*. In the same book Erich Fromm declares that values are rooted in the very condition of human existence: "the ultimate ground of values is rooted in the ultimate ground of being." And Maslow urges us to see this ground as human ground: "therapists help people every day to become more strong, virtuous, creative, kind, loving, altruistic, serene," while Pitirim Sorokin argues in the same symposium that altruistic love, as a fundamental reality of human existence, needs to be consciously and deliberately introduced into political and social affairs.

In this area of philosophical anthropology, then, Maslow's humanistic psychology is directed specifically at drawing out the positive qualities in human beings. Of course, many people do not realize that it could be possible for them to fulfill their potentialities. There are bad choosers in the quest for authenticity, and also falsifiers. Everyone, however, needs to find a sense of identity: "Since I cannot remain sane without a sense of 'I,' I am driven to do almost anything to acquire this sense."

But this humanistic psychology also links the realization of the self with interpersonal relationships and with creative, imaginative potentialities of the mind. Erich Fromm declares that the "answer to life that corresponds to the reality of human existence is conducive to mental health." To understand what is needed here, one must take "well-being" into account:

> Well-being I would describe as the *ability to be creative, to be aware, and to respond:* to be independent and fully active, and by this very fact to be one with the world. To be concerned with *being,* not with *having,* to experience joy in the very act of living—and to consider living creatively as the only meaning of life. (*New Knowledge in Human Values,* p. 163)

If living creatively is the only meaning of life, then man's need for symbolism, for cultural effort is evidently primary. And in the symposium under discussion Gyorgy Kepes declares that in Art is found "the joy of felt order:" "Our great task is to bring man in scale again with the entire horizon of nature, so that he can sense it in all its wealth and promises, harmonies and mysteries . . ." (*NK,* p. 91). What is needed is a new sense of wholeness, by accepting the deep continuities between man and nature.

Perhaps as good a definition as one might get of this existentialist position is Nicolai Berdaev's declaration:

> I am an existentialist because I believe in the priority of the subject over the object, in the identity of the knowing subject and the existing subject: I am furthermore an existing subject because I see the life of men and of the world torn by contraries, which must be faced and maintained in their tension, and which no intellectual system of a closed and complete totality, no immanentalism or optimism can resolve. I have always desired that philosophy should not be about something or somebody, but should be that very something or somebody; in other words, that it should be the revelation of the original nature and character of the subject itself. (*Dream and Reality; An Essay in Autobiography,* p. 93)

Besides this question of the recognition of subjectivity there is the question of freedom, a freedom that has to be won by the effort of learning, of disciplined, creative exploration of the world—not least by overcoming the deadness of the Galilean-Cartesian-Newtonian-Humean inheritance.

But it also indicates a manifestation of freedom that is by no means doomed to absurdity, but that finds significance in human creativity as the expression of the dynamics of the multiplicity and self-fulfillment of life itself. In politics, education, and social policy the essentials today are all missing: recognition of man as a living being in his creative role among the other beings; recognition of his consciousness; the recognition of love; and above all, delicate respect for the mystery of his existence, and the deep and grave responsibility he has toward the life from which he emerged, and that emerges from him.

Thus this book must end in an open-ended way. At the end of his book Roger Poole says that time is short; it could rather be said that time has not yet begun. That is, the whole existentialist-phenomenological movement reveals that we have been locked in attention to immediate time and the concrete moment, like Minkowski's brain-damaged patients. The current loss of hope in the future, the feeling that civilzation is in decline, is seen to be a natural consequence of natural philosophy. We need to feel the world again as a great dynamic and burning entity, of which we are the outcome, one of the highest manifestations of its inherent movement to complexity and toward higher levels of being. We may, however, whether we believe or not, feel at home in this universe, and we should feel a deep responsibility toward it, not least because of our consciousness. We should flex our creativity as a high manifestation of the emergent dynamics of live, and express man as a "radiating center."

We need to reject the naiveté of the prevalent reductionist, empiricist, objective view in favor of the new naiveté of "back to the things themselves," relinquishing the predominance of mathematical abstractions in favor of the immediate here-and-nowness of those experiences of the world which confront us.

The atmosphere of our society is one in which existence is conceived in terms of fragmented time and fragmented sensation. A creature like the common man of our time (as displayed, say, in the color supplement) has only fragmented moments of sensual gratification and so has no creative life, no life as it unfolds in the world, in the creative time of the animal as seen by philosophical biologists like Buytendijk. As Marcel says, functional modes of life and philosophy shape one another; so, in a mechanistic society man behaves as if he were a machine and also knows himself and his world in mechanistic terms, as *massemensch*. A related mechanistic knowing pervades education, not least in psychology and sociology, where the reality of *homo humanus* man as he really is, should be most of all at the center. Yet, to celebrate an essentially creative man is our only hope of escape from our present barbarism and failure of confidence in the future.

In the light of the new existentialism and phenomenology, the central and primary human needs are *meaning* and *creativity*. Both are continually being reduced by the way we live, by the ethos of our civilization, by our culture and our education, and by our general philosophy of life, which is essentially nihilistic. Even in the universities the predominant feeling is that we might (if we can afford it) build more laboratories for, say, microbiology, while the Classics and English departments might as well shrink away as a form of useless knowledge or a fusty preoccupation with a dead past.

The lesson of phenomenology, however, is that we need to return, in all humbleness, to the Greeks to discover (as Husserl makes plain) the original impulse of our civilization, to which self-fulfillment as knowledge, as man's consciousness of himself, our civilization, and our universities belong. The problems "solved" by the scientist may lead to further problems, which cannot be solved until we return to "the things themselves" and find the proper dimension of our being. "Objective" forms of knowing and their publication, and the impetus that objectivity conveys to social and political policies, may be increasingly dangerous if divorced from man's moral being by the nature of that kind of discipline. Only the quest for the *whole* truth, in the spirit of Greek thought, can save us.

It could be, from this point of view, that a return to the problems posed by the Greeks and the *telos* of their original achievement could help us to survive—hardly a useless reconsideration of Ancient Classical philosophy! But there are other disciplines in the humanities, such as English that can be enlivened by attention to the Husserlian revolution. When English comes to examine and discuss its assumptions about the nature of man and the relationship between culture and consciousness, we shall really be able to make progress in that subject. It also seems likely that the most fruitful applications of phenomenology may be in the field of cultural criticism, and the interpretation of literature, painting, and music. (See E. W. F. Tomlin *Psyche, Culture and the New Science*.)

There are also many indications for politics, and for the stance we should adopt toward the world, in the humanities and in our living.[4] Here a further useful source of definition of the new kind of philosophy I am concerned with is Gabriel Marcel's *Tragic Wisdom and Beyond* (Evanston, Ill.: Northwestern University Press, 1973). Actually, Marcel's first two chapters, "What Can Be Expected of Philosophy?" and "Responsibility of the Philosopher," would make a good starting point for the reader. In the course of the second chapter Marcel says:

Realising now that the stakes we are playing for are nothing less than the life or survival of humanity we must push our inquiry further. Only here it is necessary to be more precise, for it is not simply a question of physical survival. There are many ways for man to destroy himself or, more exactly, to dehumanise himself. Here again an untiring vigilance is required of the philosopher. But it is clearly not enough that he post a guard, so to speak, as one might do to protest a public building. *Above all it is incumbent on him, and him alone, to bring forth a conscious awareness of what man is as such. What I especially have in mind here is a philosophical anthropology like Martin Buber's.* (P. 29, emphasis added)

Marcel directly relates the need for a philosophical anthropology to our obligation to define man anew. We must uphold this new definition against the dehumanizations of our time, both in the way we live (our environment) and in the way we think.

Marcel also says that to display a bearing on the problems of life is just what philosophy has failed to do. He ends his book speaking of the purpose of wisdom as he sees it:

> In this age of absolute insecurity we live in, true wisdom lies in setting out, with prudence to be sure, but also with a kind of joyful anticipation, on the paths leading not necessarily beyond time but beyond *our* time, to where the technocrats and the statistics worshippers on the one hand, and the tyrants and torturers on the other, not only lose their footing, but vanish like mists at the dawn of a beautiful day. (P. 213)

But certainly, as I hope I have shown here, a first step is to acquaint ourselves with a revolution in philosophy that has been going on since Schelling lectured against Hegel in 1841, with Kierkegaard, Burckhardt, Engels, and Bakunin in the audience.

Notes

1. Perhaps I may suggest that the following be read: the first few chapters of *The Crisis of the European Sciences* (Evanston, Ill.: Northwestern University Press, 1970); also "Phenomenology" article in the 1929 *Encyclopedia Britannica* by Edmund Husserl; "The Relevance of Phenomenological Philosophy for Psychology" by Herbert Spiegelberg, in *Phenomenology and Existentialism*, ed. E. N. Lee and M. Mandlebaum (Baltimore: Johns Hopkins Press, 1967), pp. 219–41. Herbert Spiegelberg's two massive volumes, *The Phenomenological Movement* (The Hague: Nijhoff, 1965), are, of course, key works.

2. See the marvelous letter to Desmond Chute of artist Stanley Spencer from Salonica in March 1917, in which he says: "After fully enjoying the thought of all the varied and wonderful thoughts I am going to have during the day I get up & go & look out of the window. . . ." *Stanley Spencer: The Man, Correspondence and Reminiscences*, ed. John Rothenstein (London: Paul Elek, 1979), p. 19.

3. *Towards Deep Subjectivity*, p. 92.

4. See *Politics and the Need for Meaning*, in *Human Needs and Politics*, ed. Ross Fitzgerald (Rushcutters Bay, NSW: Pergamon Press, 1977).

Bibliography

Abbs, Peter. *Reclamations*. London: Heinemann, 1979.

Balint, Michael. *Primary Love and Psychoanalytical Technique*. London: Tavistock, 1952.

Berdayev, Nicolai. *Dream and Reality: An Essay in Autobiography*. London: Geoffrey Bles, 1950.

Binswanger, Ludwig. *Being-in-the-World*. New York: Basic Books, 1963.

———. *Introduction to the Problems of General Psychology*. Berlin: Springer, 1922.

———. *Sigmund Freud: Reminiscences of a Friendship*. New York: Grune and Stratton, 1957.

Boss, Medard. *Meaning and Content of Sexual Perversions: A Daseinsanalytic Approach to the Psychopathology of the Phenomena of Love*. New York: Grune and Stratton, 1949.

———. *Psychoanalysis and Daseinsanalysis*. New York: Basic Books, 1963.

Bowlby, John. *Child Care and the Growth of Love*. Harmondsworth: Penguin, 1953.

Brentano, Franz. Chapters translated in *Realism and the Background of Phenomenology,* edited by R. M. Chisholm. Glencoe, Ill.: Free Press, 1960.

Bretall, Robert. *A Kierkegaard Anthology*. Princeton: Princeton University Press, 1951.

Brink, Andrew. *Creativity as Repair*. Hamilton, Ontario: Cromlech Press, 1982.

———. *Loss and Symbolic Repair*. Hamilton, Ontario: Cromlech Press, 1977.

Buber, Martin. *Between Man and Man*. London: Kegan Paul, 1947.

———. "Distance and Relation." In *The Knowledge of Man,* edited by M. Friedman. London: George Allen and Unwin, 1964.

———. *I and Thou*. Edinburgh: Clark, 1937.

———. *The Philosophy of Martin Buber*. Edited by P. A. Schlipp and M. Friedman. La Salle and London: Open Court and Cambridge University Press, 1969.

Bugental, J. F. T. *The Search for Authenticity*. New York: Holt, Reinhart and Winston, 1967.

Burtt, E. A. *In Search of Philosophic Understanding*. London: George Allen and Unwin, 1967.

———. *The Metaphysical Foundations of Modern Physical Science*. London: George Allen and Unwin, 1932.

Buytendijk, F. J. J. *The Mind of the Dog*. London: Allen and Unwin, 1935.

163

————. *Pain: Its Modes and Functions.* Chicago: University of Chicago Press, 1962.

————. *Woman.* Glen Rock, N.J.: Newman Press, 1965.

Cassirer, Ernst. *An Essay on Man.* New Haven: Yale University Press, 1963.

————. *Language and Myth.* New York: Dover, 1945.

Chaloner, Len. *Feeling and Perception in Young Children.* London: Tavistock, 1963.

Collingwood, R. G. *The Idea of Nature.* Oxford: Clarendon Press, 1945.

————. *Principles of Art.* Oxford: Clarendon Press, 1938.

Curtis, B., and W. Mays, eds. *Phenomenology and Education: Self-consciousness and Its Development.* London: Methuen, 1978.

Dodds, E. R. *The Greeks and the Irrational.* Berkeley: University of California Press, 1959.

Drake, S., ed. *Discoveries and Opinions of Galileo.* New York: Doubleday, 1957.

Drury, M. O'C. *The Danger of Words.* London: Routledge and Kegan Paul, 1973.

Descartes, René. *Rules for the Direction of the Mind.* In *Philosophical Works of Descartes,* edited by E. S. Haldane and G. R. T. Ross. Cambridge: Cambridge University Press, 1950.

Dilthey, Wilhelm. *Gesammelte Schriften,* translated in *Wilhelm Dilthey,* H. A. Hodges. New York: Oxford University Press, 1944.

Dobzhansky, T. *The Biological Basis of Human Freedom.* New York: Columbia and London, 1956.

————. *The Biology of Ultimate Concern.* London: Rapp and Whiting, 1969.

Edie, James M., ed. *The Primacy of Perception.* Evanston, Ill.: Northwestern, 1964. (Contains *"The Child's Relation with Others"* by Maurice Merleau-Ponty.)

Erikson, Erik. *Childhood and Society.* New York: W. W. Norton, 1950.

Esterson, Aaron. *The Leaves of Spring.* London: Tavistock, 1965.

Fairbairn, W. R. D. *Psychoanalytical Studies of the Personality.* London: Tavistock, 1952.

Farber, Leslie H. *The Ways of the Will.* London: Constable, 1966.

Foudraine, Jan. *Not Made of Wood.* New York: Macmillan, 1974.

Frankl, Victor. *The Doctor and the Soul.* New York: Knopf, 1965.

————. *From Death Camp to Existentialism.* Boston: Beacon Press, 1963.

————. *Psychotherapy and Existentialism.* New York: Washington Square Press, 1967.

Frey-Wissling, A. *Submicroscopic Morphology of Protoplasm.* New York: Elsevier, 1953.

Friedman, Maurice. *The Knowledge of Man.* London: George Allen and Unwin, 1964.

Friedman, Maurice, and P. A. Schlipp. *The Philosophy of Martin Buber.* La Salle and London: Open Court and Cambridge University Press, 1969.

Goldstein, Kurt. *Human Nature in the Light of Psychopathology.* New York: Schocken Books, 1963.

———. *Language and Language Disturbances: Aphasic Symptoms and Their Significance for Medicine and Theory of Language.* New York: Grune and Stratton, 1948.

———. *The Organism: A Holistic Approach to Biology Derived from Pathological Data in Man.* New York: American Book, 1939.

Gould, Alan, and John Shotter. *Human Action and Its Psychological Investigation.* London: Routledge and Kegan Paul, 1977.

Grene, Marjorie. *Approaches to a Philosophical Biology.* New York: Basic Books, 1968.

———. *Dreadful Freedom: An Introduction to Existentialism.* Chicago: University of Chicago Press, 1948.

———. *The Knower and The Known.* London: Faber and Faber, 1966.

———. *Martin Heidegger.* London: Bowes and Bowes, 1957.

———. *Philosophy In and Out of Europe.* Berkeley: University of California Press, 1976.

———. *The Understanding of Nature.* Boston: D. Reidel, 1974.

Guntrip, Harry. *Personality Structure and Human Interaction.* London: Hogarth Press, 1961.

———. *Schizoid Phenomena, Object Relations and the Self.* London: Hogarth Press, 1968.

Heidegger, Martin. *Being and Time.* New York: Harper and Row, 1962.

———. *Existence and Being.* Chicago: Regnery-Gateway, 1949.

Hodgkin, R. A. *Reconnaissance on an Educational Frontier.* Oxford: Oxford University Press, 1970.

Hume, David. *A Treatise of Human Nature.* 1740. Oxford ed. Oxford: Oxford University Press, 1955.

Husserl, Edmund. *Cartesian Meditations.* The Hague: Nijhoff, 1960.

———. *The Crisis of the European Sciences and Transcendental Phenomenology.* Evanston, Ill.: Northwestern University Press, 1970.

———. *Ideas: General Introduction to Pure Phenomenology.* New York: Collier, 1962.

———. *Logical Investigations.* New York: Humanities Press, 1970.

Isaacs, Susan. *The Nursery Years.* London: Routledge, 1929.

Jaspers, Karl. *General Psychopathology.* Manchester: Manchester University Press, 1963.

———. *Man in the Modern Age.* New York: Henry Holt, 1933.

———. *The Perennial Scope of Philosophy.* New York: Philosophical Library, 1950.

Jonas, Hans. *The Phenomena of Life: Towards a Philosophical Bioloy.* New York: Harper and Row, 1966.

Jung, C. G. *Contributions to Analytical Psychology.* London: Routledge and Kegan Paul, 1928.

Kaufman, Walter A. *Nietzche: Philosopher, Psychologist, Anti-Christ.* Princeton: Princeton University Press, 1950.

Kierkegaard, Søren. *Concluding Unscientific Postscript*. Princeton: Princeton University Press, 1941.

———. *Philosophical Fragments*. Princeton: Princeton Unviersity Press, 1941.

Klein, Melanie. *Contributions to Psychoanalysis*. London: Hogarth Press, 1941.

———. *Developments in Psychoanalysis*. London: Hogarth Press, 1952.

———. *Envy and Gratitude*. London: Tavistock, 1957.

———. *New Directions in Psychoanalysis*. London: Tavistock, 1958.

———. *Our Adult Society and Its Roots in Infancy*. London: Tavistock, 1963.

———. *The Psychoanalysis of Children*. London: Hogarth Press, 1932.

Klein, Melanie, and Joan Riviere. *Love, Hate and Reparation*. London: Hogarth Press, 1938.

Kneller, George F. *Existentialism and Education*. New York: John Wiles, 1958.

Koestler, A., and J. R. Smithies, eds. *Beyond Reductionism: New Perspectives in the Life Sciences*. The Alpbach Symposium. London: Hutchinson, 1968.

Kohl, Herbert. *The Age of Complexity*. New York: New American Library, 1965.

Lauer, Quentin. *The Triumph of Subjectivity*. New York: Fordham University Press, 1958.

Laing, R. D. *The Divided Self*. London: Tavistock, 1960.

———. *Interpersonal Perception: A Theory and Method of Research*. New York: Springer, 1960.

———. *The Self and Others*. London: Tavistock, 1961.

———. *The Voice of Experience: Experience, Science and Psychiatry*. London: Tavistock, 1980.

Langer, Susanne. *Mind, An Essay in Human Feeling*. Baltimore: Johns Hopkins, 1967.

———. *Philosophical Sketches*. Baltimore: Johns Hopkins, 1962.

———. *Philosophy in a New Key*. Cambridge: Harvard University Press, 1957.

Leavis, F. R. *The Living Principle*. London: Chatto and Windus, 1978.

Lederman, E. K. *Existential Neurosis*. London: Butterworth, 1972.

Lipps, Theodore. *Die Aesthetik: Psychologie des Schönen und der Kunst*. Hamburg: Voss, 1903.

Lomas, Peter, ed. *The Case for a Personal Psychotherapy*. Oxford: Oxford University Press, 1981.

———. *The Predicament of the Family*. London: Hogarth, 1967.

———. *True and False Experience*. London: Allen Lane, 1973.

Macbeth, Norman. *Darwin Retried*. London: Garnstone, 1974.

Mach, Ernst. *Die Mechanik in ihrer Entwicklung*. Leipzig: F. A. Brockhaus, 1889.

Macmurray, John. *Reason and Emotion*. London: Faber, 1938.

———. *The Self as Agent*. London: Faber, 1935.

Marcel, Gabriel. *Being and Having*. London: Collins, 1965.

———. *The Philosophy of Existence*. London: Harvill Press, 1948.

———. *Tragic Wisdom and Beyond*. Evanston, Ill.: Northwestern University Press, 1973.

Maslow, Abraham. *Towards a Psychology of Being*. New York: Van Nostrand, 1968.

May, Rollo. *Love and Will*. New York: W. W. Norton, 1969.

———. *Man's Search for Himself*. New York: W. W. Norton, 1953.

———. *The Meaning of Anxiety*. New York: Ronald, 1950.

May, Rollo, with Ernest Angel and Henri F. Ellenberger. *Existence—A New Dimension in Psychiatry*. New York: Basic Books, 1958.

Merleau-Ponty, Maurice. *The Phenomenology of Perception*. London: Routledge and Kegan Paul, 1966.

Midgeley, Mary. *Beast and Man*. Hassocks, Eng.: Harvester, 1980.

Milner, Marion. *The Hands of the Living God*. London: Hogarth, 1969.

Monod, Jacques. *Chance and Necessity*. London: Collins, 1972.

Naevestad, Marie. *The Colours of Rage and Love*. Oslo: Universitets-forlaget, 1979.

O'Connor, D., and N. Lawrence. *Readings in Existential Phenomenology*. Englewood Cliffs, N.J.: Prentice-Hall, 1967. (Contains as essay on F. J. J. Buytendijk.)

Pivcevič, Edo. *Husserl and Phenomenology*. London: Hutchinson, 1970.

Plessner, Helmuth. *Laughing and Crying*. Evanston, Ill.: Northwestern University Press, 1970.

Polanyi, Michael. *Knowing and Being*. London: Routledge and Kegan Paul, 1969.

———. *Personal Knowledge*. London: Routledge and Kegan Paul, 1958.

———. "Science and Man." *Proceedings of the Royal Society of Medicine* 58 (1970): 975.

———. *The Tacit Dimension*. London: Routledge and Kegan Paul, 1967.

Polanyi, Michael, and Harry Prosch. *Meaning*. Chicago: University of Chicago Press, 1975.

Pols, Edward. *The Recognition of Reason*. Carbondale, Ill.: Southern Illinois University Press, 1963.

Poole, Roger. *Towards Deep Subjectivity*. London: Allen Lane, 1972.

Portmann, Adolf. *Animal Camouflage*. Ann Arbor: University of Michigan Press, 1959.

———. *Animal Form and Patterns*. London: Faber, 1952.

———. *Animals as Social Beings*. London: Hutchinson, 1961.

———. *New Paths in Biology*. New York: Harper and Row, 1961.

———. "Time in the Life of the Organism." In *Man and Time,* Papers from the Eranos Yearbooks, edited by Joseph Campbell. Princeton: Princeton University Press, 1958.

Ricouer, Paul. *Freedom and Nature*. Evanston, Ill.: Northwestern University Press, 1966.

———. *Freud and Philosophy*. New Haven: Yale University Press, 1970.

————. *Husserl: An Analysis of His Phenomenology.* Evanston, Ill.: Northwestern University Press, 1970.

Roubiczek, Paul. *Ethical Values in the Age of Science.* Cambridge: Cambridge University Press, 1969.

————. *Existentialism: For and Against.* Cambridge: Cambridge University Press, 1969.

Ruggiero, Guido de. *Existentialism: Disintegration of Man's Soul.* New York: Social Sciences, 1946.

Ruyer, Raymond. *Dieu Des Philosophes et Dieu Des Sciences.* Paris: Flammarion, 1970.

Ruytenbeck, H. *Psychoanalysis and Existential Philosophy.* New York: Dutton, 1962. (Contains as essay on F. J. J. Buytendijk on the phenomenological approach to problems of feeling and emotion.)

Ryle, G. *The Concept of Mind.* London: Hutchinson, 1949.

Sartre, Jean-Paul. *Being and Nothingness.* New York: Philosophical Library, 1956.

————. *Existentialism Is a Humanism.* New York: Philosophical Library, 1948.

————. *The Emotions, Outline of a Theory.* New York: Philosophical Library, 1948.

Schlipp, P. A., and M. Friedman. *The Philosophy of Martin Buber.* La Salle and London: Open Court and Cambridge University Press, 1969.

Schweizer, Albert. *Civilization and Ethics: The Philosophy of Civilization.* London: Adam and Charles Black, 1946.

Spiegelberg, Herbert. *The Phenomenological Movement: An Historical Introduction.* The Hague: Nijhoff, 1964.

————. *Phenomenology in Psychology and Psychiatry.* Evanston, Ill.: Northwestern University Press, 1972.

Stern, Karl. *The Flight from Woman.* London: Unwin, 1968.

Straus, Erwin, ed. *On Obsession: A Clinical and Methodological Study.* New York: Nervous and Mental Disease Monographs, 1948.

————. *Phenomenological Psychology.* New York: Basic Books, 1966.

————. *Phenomenology, Pure and Applied.* Pittsburgh, Pa.: Duquesne University Press, 1964.

————. *The Primary World of Senses.* Glencoe, Ill.: Free Press, 1963.

————. *Psychiatry and Philosophy.* New York: Springer, 1969.

Suttie, Ian D. *The Origins of Love and Hate.* London: Routledge and Kegan Paul, 1935.

Taylor, C. *The Explanation of Behaviour.* London: Routledge, 1964.

Thorpe, W. H. *Animal Nature and Human Nature.* London: Methuen, 1969.

————. *Learning and Instinct in Animals.* London: Methuen, 1963.

————. *The Uniqueness of Man.* Amsterdam and London: North-Holland Publishing Co., 1969.

Tillich, Paul. *The Courage to Be.* New Haven: Yale University Press, 1952.

Tomlin, E. W. F. *The Approach to Metaphysics.* London: Routledge and Kegan Paul, 1947.

———. *Living and Knowing.* London: Faber and Faber, 1955.

———. *Psyche, Culture and the New Science.* London: Routledge, 1985.

Towers, Bernard, and John Lewis. *Naked Ape—Or Homo Sapiens?* London: Garnstone, 1969.

Ulanov, Ann Belford. *Receiving Woman.* Philadelphia: Westminister Press, 1981.

Weiss, Paul. *Principles of Development: A Text in Experimental Embryology.* New York: U. Koft, 1939.

Whitehead, A. N. *Adventure of Ideas.* Cambridge: Cambridge University Press, 1933.

———. *Modes of Thought.* Cambridge: Cambridge University Press, 1938.

———. *Symbolism.* Cambridge: Cambridge University Press, 1927.

Wild, John. *The Challenge of Existentialism.* Bloomington: Indiana University Press, 1955.

———. *Existence and the World of Freedom.* Englewood Cliffs, N.J.: Prentice-Hall, 1963.

Winnicott, D. W. *The Child and the Family.* London: Tavistock, 1957.

———. *The Child and the Outside World.* London: Tavistock, 1957.

———. *Collected Papers: Through Pediatrics to Psychoanalysis.* London: Tavistock, 1958.

———. *The Family and Individual Development.* London: Tavistock, 1965.

———. *The Maturational Processes and the Facilitating Environment.* London: Hogarth Press, 1966.

———. *The Piggle.* London: Hogarth, 1970.

———. *Playing and Reality.* London: Tavistock, 1971.

———. *Therapeutic Consultations in Child Psychiatry.* London: Hogarth, 1971.

Wisdom, John. *Philosophy and Psychoanalysis.* Oxford: Basil Blackwell, 1952.

Index

170